Getting started in

Sales
Consulting

The Getting Started in Series

Getting Started in **Asset Allocation** by Bill Bresnan and Eric P. Gelb
Getting Started in **Online Investing** by David L. Brown and Kassandra Bentley
Getting Started in **Stocks** by Alvin D. Hall
Getting Started in **Mutual Funds** by Alvin D. Hall
Getting Started in **401(k) Investing** by Paul Katzeff
Getting Started in **Security Analysis** by Peter J. Klein
Getting Started in **Futures** by Todd Lofton
Getting Started in **Technical Analysis** by Jack D. Schwager
Getting Started in **Hedge Funds** by Daniel A. Strachman
Getting Started in **Options** by Michael C. Thomsett
Getting Started in **Real Estate Investing** by Michael C. Thomsett and
    Jean Freestone Thomsett
Getting Started in **Annuities** by Gordon M. Williamson
Getting Started in **Bonds** by Sharon Saltzgiver Wright
Getting Started in **Computer Consulting** by Peter Meyer
Getting Started in **Financial Information** by Daniel Moreau and Tracey Longo
Getting Started in **Sales Consulting** by Herman Holtz

Coming Soon . . .

Getting Started in **Online Day Trading** by Kassandra Bentley
Getting Started in **Global Investing** by Robert P. Kreitler
Getting Started in **Financial Consulting** by Ed Stone
Getting Started in **Engineering Consulting** by Stephen Wilson

Getting Started in
Sales
Consulting

Herman Holtz

John Wiley & Sons, Inc.

New York • Chichester • Weinheim • Brisbane • Singapore • Toronto

Copyright © 2000 by Herman Holtz. All rights reserved.

Published by John Wiley & Sons, Inc.

Published simultaneously in Canada.

Library of Congress Cataloging-in-Publication Data:

Holtz, Herman.
    Getting started in sales consulting / Herman Holtz.
      p.   cm.
    Includes index.
    ISBN 0-471-34812-0 (paper : alk. paper)
    1. Business consultants.   2. Selling.   I. Title.
  HD69.C6 H627 2000
  658.8—dc21   99-046350

Printed in the United States of America.

10 9 8 7 6 5 4 3 2 1

Contents

Chapter 3

Insurance and Taxes 67

Chapter 4

Pricing Your Services 83

Chapter 5

Using Lawyers, Accountants, and Other Special Services 109

Chapter 6

Building a Clientele: Marketing 127

Chapter 7

Finding Your Niches 159

Chapter 8

Selling to the Government and Proposal Writing　181

Chapter 9

Ancillary Services and Other Income Sources　205

Preface

Consulting, especially independent consulting, is a growth industry. Like all consulting specialties, sales consulting is geared closely to and driven by the increasing complexity of our society and civilization in general but more directly by newer and more technological selling systems and sales media. For example, only a few years ago, as the new personal computer was rapidly becoming an obligatory fixture in even the smallest office, a powerful new sales tool known as database marketing became available and became the subject of more than one weighty how-to tome and numerous articles on the subject. (The general objective and effect of database marketing is to make sales campaigns much more sharply focused on better-qualified prospects through building in more and more information about each individual listed in mailing lists.)

Still another, even more significant and more important development is the currently growing e-commerce (electronic commerce), or commerce conducted in cyberspace via the Internet and World Wide Web. This is a major development that will assume ever greater proportions from this time forward, and may even eclipse some of the more conventional avenues of commerce.

The more complex and diversified a field becomes, the more those involved directly and indirectly in the field need the help of specialists we call consultants, including that special class of consultants we call independent consultants. Of course, much of the increasing complexity in the sales field stems directly and indirectly from today's surging technology, new products, new industries, new methods, and new media created by that explosively growing technology. That includes the great leaps forward in some older technologies, and the effects these changes have on commerce.

Currently, independent computer consultants probably outnumber any other single class or kind of independent consultant. But there are increasing numbers of independent specialists in older fields hanging out their shingles as independent consultants, especially as modern technology changes those fields and makes many of them ever more complex. And therein, in that complexity, lies opportunity for specialists of all kinds to find new careers as independent consultants, helping clients navigate their fields successfully.

Still, not all the growth and change is directly due to technology. To at least some degree it is due to population growth, the proliferation of new products, and the increasing complexity of society in general. For example, one industry that has been growing steadily for decades, but at a greatly accelerated pace lately, is that of contract labor, the provision of temporary employees, a field that employs a great many independent consultants.

Of all the workers in our world, probably the most numerous general class are those who are salespeople of one kind or another. They work behind counters in retail establishments; they knock on doors seeking prospects; they make sales calls or initial approaches by telephone; they mail sales literature in direct mail or mail order campaigns; they join business clubs and trade associations as an aid to finding prospects and sales leads; and they are busy at conventions and other such gatherings, questing again for prospects and sales leads.

Another great indication of the significance of sales in the business world is that the most-used quantifier or qualifier employed for describing and classifying business organizations is the dollar figure of the organization's sales success. A corporation may be referred to as having sales of $900 million or being a multibillion-dollar company, or, more obliquely, described and defined with such terms as being one of the Fortune 500. The corporation's size is stated and judged by its sales figures; number of employees and other characteristics are also used, but far less dramatically. In business, sales numbers are generally accepted as the prime and most important indicators of size, success, importance, and dominance in the field of any organization.

It is thus not at all surprising that few business subjects get as much attention and coverage in print or other forms of communication and presentation as do sales and marketing. (Marketing is a separate subject, technically, but there is no question that the ultimate objective of marketing is sales.) There is no such thing as a successful business without sales success. Sales is an aggressive, proactive function of every business, even when an effort is made to sell in an almost invisible mode, as in the case of many professional practices.

In informal discussions and references, little effort is made to distinguish sales from marketing. That is understandable, since marketing success can usually be measured by sales figures. Still, in formal presentations it soon becomes clear enough that marketing is about many things, but sales is a subject unto its own, about getting orders and little else, and is certainly the main objective of marketing.

It should come as no surprise that in this era many expert salespeople are becoming independent sales consultants, and that independent sales consulting beckons more and more salespeople into that profession. Viewed overall, sales is an increasingly complex subject, one with a great many facets, old and new. When we have a close look at sales consulting, that complexity soon becomes apparent. The enormous diversity in sales media, industries, methods, objectives, and philosophies is inevitable, given the enormous diversity of commerce, all of which is referred to and covered by the activities known as sales. The differences are along at least four broad lines of diversity:

1. Nature of the product or class of goods to be sold.
2. Typical or most commonly used sales methods and media.
3. Different classes of prospects and buyers.
4. Type of services you will offer as a sales consultant.

Even that is just the beginning, and these categories are so general that they are almost arbitrary. Each of those categories can be subdivided several times and, moreover, the subdivisions can be divided again. (In fact, one problem for the beginning sales consultant is choosing a field of sales services to offer.) And so sales consulting presents the special problem that there are so many variables and so many alternatives that the sales consultant must choose his or her specialties carefully and not attempt to sell him- or herself as someone who can do it all and is equally expert in all.

One thing that is as predictable and inevitable as death and taxes is change, and one thing that change brings with equal inevitability is greater complexity. In the sales field, a great change has come about by the introduction of selling in cyberspace—via the Internet and other online channels—which has itself swiftly become a specialized sales field. There are few fields today in which a consultant can do it all with equal skill and effectiveness, and sales is certainly not one of those few.

In fact, before you make your decisions in selecting or reselecting the niche or niches of sales consulting that you choose for your own as your area of specialization, you must decide just how specialized it is to be. That is, how narrow your field of specialization. Will you opt for a single niche or for two or more related niches? Or will you start with several niches and narrow the field as experience dictates? (That is one of the subjects we will be discussing in these pages.)

You will have to address several questions in making these decisions: Will you serve client needs in software sales, hardware sales, or both? High-tech products, low-tech products, or both? Product sales, service sales, or both? Direct sales, indirect sales, or both? Small-tag items, big-tag items, or both? Will you support clients in direct marketing, retailing, wholesaling, or all? In selling through manufacturers' reps, sales employees, or both? Conventional advertising? Special promotions? Both?

On the other hand, who will be the prospects you see as most likely to be your clients and markets? Consumers generally? Men? Women? Both? Manufacturers and original sources? Wholesalers? Retailers? Brokers?

What services will you offer as a sales consultant? Analysis of the client's sales needs and problems and recommendations to solve problems and satisfy needs? Development of overall sales plans and strategies? Preparation of sales materials? Training of salespeople? Design and management of special public relations (PR) events? Trade show management and promotion?

Even if you were able and willing to handle all the situations and do all of these things, it is almost impossible to sell an all-encompassing capability to any client. The typical client believes that his or her situation is special and different, requiring experience and capability matching the client's view of what it takes to sell the client's products or service. Thus, the client is likely to dismiss you arbitrarily as a charlatan, or at the least unsuitable to his or her needs, if you profess to be able to handle any and all sales needs. It is essential that you decide what services are best for your purposes (i.e., those that best represent your experience and maximum capabilities, those you prefer performing). But are those also the services you are likely to be best able to sell to prospective clients? That is, of course, a most important consideration, and there are a number of factors to consider, factors that will be discussed here.

All of these considerations do not necessarily mean that you must restrict your market excessively. Quite the contrary, there are consulting services that have such broad application that you can fit them appropriately to quite a large portion of the entire spectrum. That might include, for example, specializing in delivering inspirational seminars and speeches, and virtual prayer meetings on how to be a dynamic salesperson. There are writer-consultants who specialize in creating sales materials, such as those needed in direct marketing. There are public relations experts who can handle all your needs in that area of special promotions to stimulate sales. Even so, the odds are against your being able to sell yourself as equally able in all of these fields.

In this age of the specialist, clients will generally resist any claim to being able to do it all, even if you could present a track record to support the claim. You usually cannot base a successful sales argument on facts, at least not on your own opinion of what are the facts; you sell to the client's view of the facts, the client's perception of truth. If you can do it all and wish to offer your services to do it all, you need to subdivide your field into a suitable number of believable specialties and prepare suitable sales literature for each. You can't offer the same services to a manufacturer of bicycles that you offer to a groceries wholesaler and expect to be accepted by both. These are subjects that merit the extended discussions and closer examinations you will find later in these pages.

HERMAN HOLTZ

Consulting: What Is It?

Sometimes a term is more clearly explained by describing what it is not than by attempting to explain what it is.

WHAT CONSULTING IS AND IS NOT

It has long been difficult to define or explain consulting in a way that satisfies everyone, for several reasons. One is that *consulting* has become a most general term, applied to many kinds of custom services. Another is that there is a difference of opinion about what a consultant does or ought to do. It is thus necessary for us to settle on some definition/explanation, if we are to communicate. Here is one we shall use here, a brief definition that, I believe, reflects reality, not opinions:

Consulting is not itself a profession, but a special way to practice a profession, any profession.

If you are now an expert salesperson or sales manager and you become a sales consultant, you are still that same *sales* expert, even with your new title, and you rely on that same expert knowledge, skills, and experience you have used in the past to do what you do every day. Now, however, you use those skills and that knowledge in a much different way: You use them to help others—

consulting
a special way to practice a profession by using one's special skills and knowledge to help clients solve problems.

sales
converting prospects to clients and winning contracts.

1

clients—with their own sales needs. That may be advising clients, training sales staffs, troubleshooting ailing sales campaigns, designing new sales programs, organizing sales departments, developing sales strategies, or otherwise applying your skills and knowledge to assist clients in some way to create, troubleshoot, or otherwise improve their sales programs. The service you provide clients is known as consulting.

> Consulting is not itself a profession, but a special way to practice a profession, any profession, using your expert knowledge of that profession to support a client in reaching his or her own goals.

WHAT IS SALES CONSULTING?

 **sales consulting**
using expert sales skills and knowledge to help clients solve sales problems.

With this premise accepted, it is easy to define *sales consulting* as continuing to practice those sales skills and functions you have been practicing, but in a different mode, as a service to help other salespeople and executives in solving sales problems and achieving greater success in their sales programs.

One thing that is common to all consulting is that it is a service that must be sold, as any service must be sold. That requires an understanding of the client's reasons for seeking consulting help, of course, and there is more than one school of thought on that subject.

Many people perceive consulting as purely a problem-solving service for clients who are unable to solve the problems for themselves because they do not have enough expertise in the relevant fields, need the objectivity of someone outside the organization, or want the objectivity and reassurance of some outside expert's opinion.

That perception of consulting as purely one of problem solving is partly true: It is the nominal and traditional definition of consulting. Clients do call on consultants for help when they have problems that they believe can be solved only through the services of experts. But the problems clients want solved are not always problems arising from the client's lack of special knowledge or experience. In many cases, the client knows how to solve the problem, but needs outside help to provide the solution the client knows to be the right solution. In fact, many clients know exactly what they are doing and already have successful sales programs, but feel a need for *ancillary services* of some kind to augment their own resources, such as additional "hands and feet" to supplement their own capability. Thus many clients hire one or more consultants who become, in fact, temporary employees. (The latter is especially the case in this era of high employment and relative difficulty in hiring enough qualified help.)

On the other hand, there are many prospective clients who need help but will not take the initiative in seeking help, and may not even know that there are sales consultants available to help them solve problems and improve sales performance. Thus, many sales executives do not feel a need for consulting help until they learn somehow that such service is available. As an *independent consultant*, you must therefore be aware of this truth and recognize that you need a *marketing* program that will reach out to prospective clients. It must reach both those who know that they need help and those who do not yet know that they need help or that such help is readily available.

ancillary services
additional consulting services such as publishing newsletters and special reports, and presenting seminars.

independent consultant
one who practices his or her career activity in a special mode, helping clients solve problems for which the consultant is especially fitted as an expert specialist.

Your first sales requirement will be to sell your own services as a consultant. Remember that prospective clients include those who will not feel a need for your services until they learn that such services are available and what those services can do for them, so your marketing program should be educational, as well as persuasive.

marketing
all activities leading to and including making sales.

As a sales consultant you must apply your own sales skills to win clients. Ironically, it may be that although you are a sales expert, you do not know how to go about marketing a consulting service—your sales experience most likely is in a field quite different from that of selling professional services. Selling a service of any kind, even a nonprofessional kind, is not the same as selling shoes or automobiles, and your own sales skills may thus not be appropriate for selling consulting services. So do not be dismayed if you find it necessary to seek help yourself in learning how to market your new sales consulting practice.

That you may find this the case ought not to be surprising, given the enormous diversity of sales specialties. It is impractical, essentially impossible, to try to be equally experienced and expert in all sales fields—direct and indirect, wholesale and retail, products and services, big-tag and small-tag items, via all communications media, and in all the other niches and avenues of sales specialization. You will eventually come to understand what is needed and be able to adapt your sales know-how to your own marketing need. In the meanwhile, consider just these few major services and functions in which sales consultants concentrate and in which you might offer services to clients:

seminar
a special training session involving one or more speakers for a period of not more than a few days.

proposal
an offer, usually (but not always) written, to enter into contract, presenting a plan and price.

- ✔ Training and *seminars* (general sales training).
- ✔ Specialized training and seminars (e.g., direct mail, wholesale, retail).
- ✔ Writing general marketing materials (brochures, sales letters, etc.).
- ✔ Writing specialized sales materials, such as *proposals*.
- ✔ Analysis of client's situation and recommendations.
- ✔ Design of complete sales programs.
- ✔ Development of sales plans.

That listing does not describe all the ways in which sales consultants specialize, of course. Most will quite naturally specialize in the kinds of sales and types of products in which they can claim direct sales experience and accomplishments, such as the following:

- ✔ Hard goods.
- ✔ Soft goods.
- ✔ Specific types of products.
- ✔ Services.
- ✔ Intangibles.
- ✔ Consumables.
- ✔ High tech.

Even that list that does not describe all the variants possible. There are also the sales media and methodologies to consider:

- ✔ Direct response.
- ✔ Retail.
- ✔ Wholesale.
- ✔ Special promotions.

> Despite being a sales expert in some field or sales function, you may have to acquire new sales skills suitable for selling consulting services, and even venture into other services and specialties than you pursued in the past.

Specialization can go much further than that, of course, even into the kinds of merchandise with which the consultant is most familiar and most experienced. The client who manufactures and sells cosmetics, for example, is likely to insist on a consultant whose experience is in selling cosmetics, and may even insist that the experience must be in selling cosmetics at the wholesale or retail level. (One consultant I met worked one day each week for a department store charged with organizing the cosmetic department, recommending new sales programs, and otherwise providing direct supervision and management of cosmetic sales on a weekly basis.)

It's not at all unusual for clients to believe that success in selling their line requires special know-how, and only those with that sales experience are qualified to participate in their sales program. That may be carrying specialization a shade too far, but the principle is valid: No one can be expected to be equally expert in all areas or even experienced in all areas and all sales niches. However, the need to confine yourself to some relatively narrow range of specialties also stems from two other considerations. One is that of client perceptions, that clients will generally not accept what they see as generalization in a consultant. The very idea of consulting implies a high degree of specialization, and clients usually expect consultants to be well-defined experts, and so must claim a suitably narrow range of expert skills.

But still another consideration is that of effective marketing. Many of the sales niches represent markets that are specialized enough to be different from all others, and different clients thus have different problems to solve and different services they require. Moreover, sales techniques and functions change, as in the case of database marketing and its impact on direct marketing. So you must also be able to keep up with what is new and changing in your special sales field. It would be extremely difficult for you to market your services with equal effectiveness to all fields—to wholesalers, manufacturers, direct marketers, and chain store retailers, for example. You must therefore choose with great care those *market niches* in which you not only believe yourself expert enough to be an able consultant, but have credentials enough to be so perceived by prospective clients, and be up with the latest ideas in that field. (Of course, the

 market niches
special market segments selected as targets because of some distinctive characteristic.

niches must also be large enough market segments to be worth pursuing.)

As a consultant, you therefore need a marketing program that will reach out to prospective clients, both those who are aware of their needs and in the market for help and those who do not yet know that they need help or that help is so readily available.

> A consultant must be a specialist, and it is important not only to have a well-defined specialty, but to be sure that the client understands clearly, in the client's terms, what that specialty is and what you can do for him or her.

In that respect, establishing a consulting practice and winning clients is the same as in all selling in that you must understand and satisfy clients' needs in terms of the clients' perceptions, not your perceptions—*positioning* yourself in such a way as to be in reasonable conformity with the client's perceptions. (You must make an effort to gain some understanding of the client's perceptions.) But even all of this is only a partial answer to "What is consulting?" because it does not cover the many ways in which a consultant may serve a client or in which the client expects to be served. The term "consulting" is not at all easy to define in that regard, and we should have a clear understanding of what it means, in addition to the brief definition given earlier, at least for the purposes of communicating clearly in this book.

positioning
shaping your image to how you wish clients to perceive you and what you offer—what you *do* for clients.

WHAT DOES A CONSULTANT DO?

Despite the many ways in which consultants work and the great variety of services they provide clients, many purists persist, even today, in seeing consulting as problem solving, as noted earlier. It is true enough in many cases. In medicine, for example, the consultant is often a medical specialist who is called on to render a diagnosis in his or her special field, furnish a second opinion, or confirm a diagnosis already made, and may or may not be called on to render a "doing" service, such as surgery or other treatment.

On the other hand, while it is true that a client always calls on a consultant for services to solve a problem of some kind, the problem is not necessarily a technical one nor even a difficult one to state and understand. There should be no automatic assumption that the client does not know how to solve the problem. The client may very well know what the problem is and how it must be solved, but require help nevertheless, for any of many possible reasons: A client with a temporary need for more staff than he or she has available may call for help in the form of additional qualified specialists, and it is not uncommon to refer to those professional temporaries as consultants. (A more recent term for consultants who prefer to hire out as temporaries is *contract professionals*.) There is a very large market today for such consulting services— that is, for technical, professional, and paraprofessional temporaries of all kinds. For several reasons, that market continues to grow rapidly, and is a great resource for both independent consultants and organizations that are for-profit, nonprofit, and even government agencies. All of these often hire temporaries, sometimes in large numbers and for rather long-term situations. (It can be much less costly in several ways to hire temporaries for long-term assignments. Many temporaries remain in that status with the same client for five years and even longer.)

> **contract professional** individual who normally works as a temporary.

THE CLIENT-CONSULTANT RELATIONSHIP

This brings up another often misunderstood aspect of consulting. Clients want your counsel, but in most cases, consulting is more than problem solving and advice giving: Most clients want specific services and specific results. The client in direct mail who hires a sales consultant usually wants the consultant to design and write or at least guide the design and writing of the package to be mailed. (As a proposal consultant, for example, I always write much of the proposal, often edit and manage all of it, and in many cases do all the work of creating the entire proposal myself.) So consulting is more than counseling; it is also doing. This is important to understand if you are to satisfy your clients' needs and, even before you reach that stage, make it clear in your marketing that you offer such a complete service.

That presents a potential problem because the Internal Revenue Service has in the past made it difficult for a consultant to be accepted as an *independent contractor (IC)* if he or she works on a client's *premises* full time, adheres to the client's work schedule, or otherwise fails the IRS's *20 questions* designed to validate or refute the consultant's claim to status as an independent contractor. This has stimulated the growth of consultants in the role of contract professional or temporary employee, so that the provision of contract professionals has grown steadily as a busy industry of its own. You may thus call yourself an independent consultant, but as such you may be an independent contractor or a contract professional, or even both.

independent contractor (IC) consultant who enters into contracts directly with clients, rather than via brokers, and works as a 1099 rather than as a W-2.

Usually, you will be employed as either an independent contractor or a temporary employee. In both cases, you may contract with or be employed by either the client or an organization providing your services to the client.

premises a physical location.

A SOLUTION TO THE PROBLEM

There is a way around the problem of the IRS and its 20 questions, if you prefer to be an independent contractor but have a problem meeting the IRS's requirements posed

20 questions twenty points the IRS uses to judge whether a consultant is or is not legally a temporary employee.

corporation
artificial entity, recognized by the state, with certain benefits, such as limited liability, and certain obligations, such as paying taxes and keeping records.

W-2
form required to be issued to employees; term used to designate working status of consultant as temporary employee, rather than independent contractor.

by those questions. You can incorporate yourself and become the employee of your own *corporation*, assigned to consulting work for a given client. This can be an effective shield against the IRS, with its 20 questions and tendency to judge independent contractors to be actually temporary employees. Note the words "can be," because this arrangement imposes certain conditions. The IRS reserves the right to verify that you are, indeed, a valid corporation by checking to see whether you comply fully with all proper corporate practices, including the following:

✔ Deposit all receipts to the corporation's account and pay yourself from that account as a W-2 employee.

✔ File corporate tax returns, as well as personal tax returns.

✔ Issue stock to yourself.

✔ Follow all corporate formalities, such as these:

    ✔ Hold annual meetings.

    ✔ Keep corporate records.

    ✔ Write resolutions, as necessary.

You must follow this scrupulously, if you want to be sure that you are in a position to survive an audit, should the IRS wish to investigate the legitimacy of your corporation. If you fail to do these things, the IRS can claim that yours is not a legitimate corporation and so deny you status as an independent contractor.

You must decide, therefore, if you are willing to accept the additional work and obligations of incorporation to ensure your status as an independent contractor.

As we proceed through the pages to follow, we will revisit some of these areas to discuss them at much greater length. Bear the following in mind, however, as you proceed: A premise upon which this book is based is that you are experienced and expert in some kind of sales—direct mail, wholesale, personal services, big-tag items, department store, or other—but not all. Thus some of the explanations and examples you encounter may seem too basic or too obvious to be worth reading, while others may be completely strange and new to you. In any case, it is not the goal of this book to teach marketing and sales, but rather how to specialize as a consultant in those sales practices and methodologies you know and can employ in a client's behalf.

1

Founding Your Business

You need a base of operations, as any business does. Independent consulting is a small business, of course, and requires the facilities of any small business.

ORGANIZATION AND STRUCTURE

There are a number of things you must do in setting up any business venture, even a small one that you fly by the seat of your pants, such as an independent consulting practice. But we are now poised on the threshold of the twenty-first century, in the midst of an unprecedented technology era that is truly revolutionary when viewed from the perspective of those decades that immediately preceded World War II, that natural dividing line between great eras. The small-business methods of the past, especially those of the earlier decades of the twentieth century, will not serve even our modest business needs, not even for the first days of a new, independent consulting practice. In what now appears to those of us who grew up in the 1920s and 1930s to have been greatly simpler times, a cigar box full of bills and receipts served a great many of the small business owners as their accounting systems. Of course, that will not do today, in this modern era of supertechnology for everyone. Nor is it truly difficult, in

13

accounting
keeping track of all the money, in and out of the venture, and using that information as a basis for monitoring the health of the business and making management decisions, as well as paying taxes.

local area network (LAN)
interconnected computers within a building or suite of offices.

these times of high-tech equipment and methods readily available to all, to institute a classic *accounting* system for even the smallest independent enterprise. The equipment is here, the costs are manageable, automation is advanced so that learning is not difficult, and if there are modern Luddites at work, they are not much in evidence as yet.

Marketing today is also a much different project than in those earlier decades, and requires a greatly different methodology than distributing handbills or advertising in the morning newspaper. Even a small business today must be operated as though it were a large business, with the formal, modern systems that have made this possible. Too, there are many special considerations in marketing a professional service such as consulting that we shall have to discuss at some length.

Fortunately, today's technology not only allows you to emulate larger businesses, but actually facilitates your doing so. Where the large firm may have dozens of computers, you have only one and need only one, presumably, although many very small businesses have more than one computer today, and may even have them interconnected with a *local area network (LAN)*. But even a single modern desktop computer can do for you what all those dozens of interconnected computers do for the large company. No matter how small your venture, you need and can have all the normal features and facilities of any business: dedicated office/working space, a formal accounting system, furniture and office equipment, insurance, stationery, telephone service, and an effective marketing program to win clients and contracts.

That will necessitate and include at least some sales literature, such as business cards, perhaps a brochure or two, and such other advertising matter as a sales letter to announce the establishment of and explain your sales consulting services, invite inquiries, and perhaps offer free initial consultation and estimates, as many consultants do. But there is much more than that to marketing your services, in the full sense of marketing, and we will come to that and discuss it in detail a bit later. But first let's consider several important matters that must be decided on and settled up front—upon founding your consulting practice, that is. Here are three things you need to attend to at once:

1. Decide on the form of your business organization.
2. Establish the name of your organization.
3. Create a home base for your organization.

FORM OF YOUR BUSINESS ORGANIZATION

The form and legal status of your practice will be the consequence of how you choose to organize and operate your business—your personal preference, for you have a number of choices. Your business organization can take any of three general forms or structures. It can be you alone as a sole proprietor, a partnership, or a corporation. The simplest form is the *sole proprietorship*, and the majority of independent consulting practices begin as sole proprietorships, although some change later on to some other form.

sole proprietorship the sole ownership and control of a business venture, with all assets and liabilities those of the proprietor.

The Sole Proprietorship

As a sole proprietor, the business is you and you are the business, very much like the vanishing mom-and-pop stores that were once urban fixtures on countless corners in the old residential neighborhoods. That is, you own all assets of the business personally. You are personally responsible and liable for all debits, deficits, and other liabilities of the business. You make all business decisions and you answer to no one for them (except, perhaps, to a spouse), although you may use other consultants or business coaches to advise you and help you reach decisions.

The Partnership

Some independent consultant practices are launched as partnerships of two or more individuals. This is not exactly uncommon, but it is the exception rather than the rule. Exactly how much of the business each partner owns, what the authority and responsibility of each partner are, and all the other details regarding who does what and who owns what vary widely from one firm to another, and must be worked out by the partners in each case. Partners are often individuals who are on good terms with each other through business relationships or who are old friends, and they tend to start with a verbal partnership *agreement*, at least partly out of fear that calling for a written agreement may suggest a lack of trust and strain the relationship from the beginning. That is usually a mistake, regardless of the personal relationship. It is always best to operate in a completely businesslike manner. If you are going into a partnership, it is wise for each partner to have his or her own lawyer, and to be joined in business with a formal partnership agreement drawn up by the lawyers. If you each have a lawyer, no doubt the lawyers will agree that a written agreement is a necessity, and it will probably save you a lot of grief later by ensuring that your personal interests are protected.

> **agreement** verbal or written statement between two or more parties that can become a legally binding contract if it meets the five standard requirements.

> If you go into partnership in starting a consulting practice, be completely businesslike and have a partnership agreement drawn up by a lawyer. It's a wise move for each partner to have his or her own lawyer present to negotiate the agreement.

Incorporation

The corporation is a legal entity, and when you incorporate, it is the corporation, not you personally, that becomes owner of the practice and all assets, the responsible entity for all liabilities (with a few exceptions), and the manager/decision maker. The corporation also becomes your employer and pays you a salary, commissions, or fees, according to whatever you decide to make your conditions of employment. If you hold all offices, you confer with yourself to reach decisions.

Most independent consultants who incorporate do so after they have been in practice for a while as a sole proprietorship. Usually, when they do, they opt for a simple, close corporation. You would normally make yourself president of the corporation, and you may wish to appoint family members to other corporate posts, as many consultants do. (In some states, you can hold all the posts yourself, and you may wish to consider that, if it is an available option in your state of incorporation.) You can incorporate in any state. At one time, even the largest corporations chose to incorporate in Delaware, then known as the state most friendly to corporations. Today, it has become easy and inexpensive to incorporate in most states, so more and more consultants choose to incorporate in their home states. (If you opt to incorporate in a state other than your own, you will have to register in your own state as a foreign corporation and arrange to have someone represent your corporation in the state where it was incorporated. Normally, that is an expense and paperwork that can be avoided by incorporating in your own state.)

In most states now, you can usually handle your own incorporation as a simple and routine matter (often only a one- or two-page form), although you may prefer to have a lawyer handle it for you, if you decide to incorporate. It would probably be wise, however, to discuss this with your accountant, if you use an accounting firm to handle your books and taxes, and possibly with an attorney as well, even if you do your own incorporation. Each of those other two specialists will have something to add for your understanding and consideration.

A word of caution: If you decide to incorporate, do it for the right reasons. Don't make the mistake of thinking that an "Inc.," "Corp.," or "Ltd." following your name will add to your prestige and bring you more clients. Most will hardly notice that, much less give it any thought. You may run into an occasional client who will do business only with corporations, or be impressed by such status, but that is a basic business decision of theirs and has nothing to do with how they regard you professionally. On the other hand, if incorporating will win you one or more major clients worth having, that may itself be ample reason for incorporating. (I incorporated originally to help solve a special tax problem, which is also a valid reason for incorporating.)

> As one of the first steps, you will have to decide for yourself what your legal form of organization is to be, but you can always start in one way and make changes later, after you have gained some experience and gained a better appreciation of the pros and cons of each form.

D/B/A: Doing Business As

If you are going to start as a sole proprietorship or as a partnership, you can trade under your own personal name(s), and you then need do nothing special except to check and see if you need a local mercantile license of some sort. If you are going to use some trade name, such as Superior Consulting Services, that makes you a *d/b/a* firm, one that is *doing business as* whatever the fictitious name is. You must register that name as required by your state or local fictitious names statute. That usually requires that you fill out a form identifying yourself as the person or persons doing business as Superior Consulting Services, and that you advertise this in an English-language newspaper or in the *Legal Intelligencer*, a journal for the legal profession. However, you must check to see what the legal requirements are in your state and county to operate as a d/b/a (doing business as) business. They may vary in detail from one

d/b/a (doing business as) organization or individual doing business under an assumed name.

place to another. You can, of course, consult a lawyer, but you can often get all the information you need from the county clerk or other official.

NAMING YOUR BUSINESS ORGANIZATION

The d/b/a legal requirements are one consideration in choosing a name, but there are other things to consider. You should not choose a name casually. It may seem unimportant at first, when you are preparing to hang out your shingle (launch and announce your practice), but you may regret later not having given the matter more thought when you had the chance. One reason that the name you choose is important is that it affects your *professional image* and therefore your marketing effectiveness. Decide in advance how you want prospects to perceive you professionally on first impression, which is what your business name will create. Many newcomers to consulting decide to conjure up names that they think will be impressive and suggest that they are sizable firms, rather than individuals. That is why newcomers may choose a name along the lines of Nationwide Consulting Services or invent what they think will be a highly distinctive and impressive name suggesting science and technology, such as TechnoTrends Consulting Specialists, Inc.

professional image
how you are generally perceived as a professional expert who consults.

A mistake some make is to choose a name that they think sounds impressive or highly technical but which tells the average prospective client nothing about you, who and what you are, and what you offer clients. You may think that a name such as TechnoSell, Inc., is a clever and attention-getting way of letting people know that you are a sales consultant, but the name does not really convey that. It would be difficult to determine just what message that name would deliver. Far better, I think, would be something simple and direct, such as Sales Support Service or even Sales Troubleshooters.

On the other hand, you may think that using your own name, Jack Jones Associates, encourages a closer and more friendly relationship with clients and is thus a plus for marketing. Or your name may already be well known in your industry and you believe that you will therefore enjoy a distinct marketing advantage in making yourself easily identifiable as an independent consultant. Consider all such pluses and minuses when choosing a name. Try to plan carefully and be sure, when you make a decision, that you have no doubts about it. To change your business name later can cost you clients and considerable expense, so it is not advisable. It is far wiser to take your time in thinking things out. Try, then, to select a name for permanency, one you expect to be able to live with for a long, long time. There is ample precedent for simple names. One of the larger and older firms in temporary staffing of engineering and technical positions is H. L. Yoh & Company, for example, and Booz, Allen & Hamilton Inc. is a sizable consulting firm. General Electric Company was a good enough name to found one the major U.S. corporations.

> Give ample thought to choosing a business name. It can be important to your success in conveying the right message and first impression of your services and your professional stature. Simplicity is often the best choice and rarely a bad choice.

Too Definitive a Name

In choosing a name for your business, you may wish the name to help prospective clients get a clear identification of your main specialty—direct mail, for example. That is a good idea if you are quite sure that you have chosen the specialty you will want to keep and offer permanently. But suppose that you are trying out specialties experimentally to discover which specialty is most easily marketed or you have chosen a specialty that later proves to be the wrong one for you, and you want to change it. Or suppose you wish to broaden your field, or you wish to leave the door open to add to or change your main specialties. You may have already typecast yourself as a direct mail consultant and have difficulty later in persuading clients and prospective clients to view you as a source of help in other sales specialties than direct mail. It is surprising how clients will decide that whatever kind of work you did for them in the past or were known for originally is your chosen specialty, and they will look elsewhere when they have a slightly different kind of work, even though you have tried to make it clear that you handle that work, too. (It will also be difficult to change your business name without confusing existing clients and possibly losing some of them as a result.) Consider all of these factors in choosing a name for your firm.

> Think carefully when choosing a name for your business. There are several factors to consider, and it will not be easy to change your mind and your business name later, after you are established.

Naming Your Specialty

Before you make your final decision on what you wish to name your business, you might make yet another analysis, an analysis from another viewpoint: Consider the possible names, not as describing your business, but as describing *you*. Every independent consultant is a specialist, of course, usually in a broad field in which there are many specialties. As a consultant, my broad field was marketing, and my marketing specialty was selling to the government, or winning government *contracts*, but I promoted myself as a proposal-writing specialist. The fact is that in helping clients develop proposals that win contracts, and in teaching the writing of winning proposals, I deal with all the aspects of government marketing, of which proposal writing is only one element, albeit a most important one. So why do I not give myself top billing as a government marketing expert, a

 contract agreement, verbal or written, meeting five conditions required to be legally binding contract.

much broader description of who and what I am, rather than as a proposal-writing expert, a relatively narrow view of who and what I am?

I could rationalize an explanation of that decision, of course, but the truth is I can't offer a logical explanation of why I thought "proposal consultant" more powerfully appealing than "government marketing consultant" or "government contracts consultant." It was an instinct based on my experience and my knowledge of what significance proposal writing has within organizations for which government contracts are the major objective of their marketing programs. That is, a large percentage of top-level people in government contracting businesses have some firsthand experience in proposal writing, or have in some way come to understand what proposals are and their significance in the company's marketing program. Or they may be well aware of how difficult it is normally to find in-house staff with which to staff a proposal-writing effort or, even worse, someone in-house who can manage a proposal-writing effort. That tends strongly to give proposal writing a special significance and importance, almost an emotional element. That is, it enables executives to identify with proposal writing. That is an excellent way to get attention and arouse interest. If you can find some such element in your own situation, it will help you greatly in finding the name or term most likely to strike a nerve with prospective clients.

YOUR BUSINESS ORGANIZATION'S HOME BASE

An Office at Home

By far, the majority of independent consultants work from offices in their own residences. A *home office* offers obvious benefits in minimizing start-up costs by taking care of some items, such as telephone service and often such office equipment as a computer and printer. It also minimizes *overhead* and other costs, and offers you tax benefits. Briefly, you can deduct as a business expense the cost of

home office
office in your home, using dedicated space.

overhead
indirect costs such as rent, heat, light, and indirect labor.

the space you use for an office in your home if you dedicate the space, using it for business purposes only and making the dedication clear by using a separate room or partitioned space. Prorate the cost of the space in rent or mortgage costs for tax purposes. Do the same for any other facilities you share with your business—telephone, automobile, computer, and other such items. Doing this helps greatly in maintaining a low overhead rate, and that gives you an advantage in marketing, of course. However, if you use the kitchen table to compile a mailing or other business use, you are not entitled to deduct anything for that. The space you write off must be dedicated to the business.

I started with an expensive suite of offices in a prestigious downtown office building. After several years of battling traffic, paying far too much to park my automobile during the day, worrying about two rents, two telephone bills, and other duplicated costs (plus the costs of lunches in trendy restaurants nearby), and enduring the high-stress drive into the crowded city every morning, I moved to an office at home, where I have been since with no regrets. It was a good move, and one my clients understood and approved. (I had been just a bit apprehensive about that and what the move would do to my professional image, but I was reassured by clients who perceived that I was reducing overhead in a thoroughly businesslike way, and that they would receive some benefit from that.)

> An office in your home offers several major advantages, but there may be problems also. Consider your needs and possible alternatives with great care in weighing all the pros and cons before making a firm decision.

 zoning laws statutes forbidding conduct of business in areas zoned by local government as for residential use only, as in private homes in such areas.

Zoning laws generally prohibit running a business in your home, especially forbidding advertising signs of any kind and excessive traffic to and from your home, so most consultants are discreet about minimizing traffic in and out of their homes and avoiding signs and other indications that you are using a residential location for business. Zoning boards, however, do not go out to look for violations. They normally act to enforce zoning codes only when someone makes a complaint of an alleged violation and thus compels the zoning people to check and act. (I have personally had some unpleasant experience with this problem, caused by a spiteful neighbor.) So be careful to operate your office at home quietly and do nothing to publicize the fact that your home is also a business location. Many consultants use a post office box as a return address for mail as another discreet measure. (A recent newsletter from the U.S. Postal Service suggests this as a wise business move for an at-home business.) Should you require frequent visits of clients to your office, or if visits from clients are only occasional but are not convenient to conduct in your office at home, you can make arrangements to meet over lunch or for the rental of pooled office and conference space, such as is available in most cities. (Check your Yellow Pages for office services, where such facilities are advertised.)

Office Systems and Procedures

Of course, an accounting system is a must for any business, as remarked on earlier. For one thing, the IRS demands that you be able to present records if asked (i.e., if audited). These can be invoices, bills, and receipts piling up on a crowded desk, after the manner of small neighborhood merchants of decades ago, and still satisfy the law, but such primitive systems do not satisfy the requirements of running a successful business, and you can't handle government or commercial contracts properly without a proper accounting system. (For many government contracts, the responsible contracting officer will actually want to examine your office and check out the suitability of your accounting system to provide fully detailed and accurate reports.)

On this subject, take note: Although you need to

maintain accounting records for tax purposes, that is not the main purpose of accounting. The real purpose of accounting is for your own direct benefit as a key management tool. Accurate and easily visible accounting exposes and reveals the most important truths of costs, marketing, sales, and profits or the lack of profits. The most important requirement of accounting in that respect is that the key figures be highly visible: You should be able to monitor those key numbers as frequently as you wish, as indicators of how you are doing as a manager. Ideally, you should be able to monitor key figures almost continuously. The numbers should alert you to problems and opportunities at an early time, before serious damage can result from problems and while you can exploit opportunities revealed or suggested by the records.

> Never underestimate the importance of your accounting system. It is your chief management tool, revealing the state of your business at all times. Choose it and use it with great care to gain maximum advantage from it.

Keeping your own accounts is not the most efficient use of your time and might only add to your problems. On the other hand, using the services of a local accountant makes it difficult to monitor your accounts very closely. I solved the dilemma eventually, after several tries, by keeping the books myself. ("Books" is a euphemism: In a simple system, there is only one book, a ledger for all accounts, with sections for the diary or day journal, income/receivables, debits/payables, and other, related records.) That is a simple enough job for a small business, so the figures are always there before me in a single volume. A public accounting firm handles my taxes and reports. Actually, my spouse keeps the book, pays the bills, and generally runs my business office. I am sure that many consultants have similar arrangements. Of course, today you can use a simple computer program to handle most of the accounting work on your own personal computer (PC). Again, many spouses can and do handle this because the accounting programs designed especially for small businesses are almost automatic.

Above all, remember always that you and you alone make the decisions. Accountants, lawyers, consultants, friends, and relatives advise you and express their opinions and recommendations (most will, of course), but only you can and should then make the decisions, and you must be sure that it is only you doing so. Consider all the advice offered, ask as many questions as you like, educate yourself in what you need to know to make sound decisions, but then insist that only you can and will make those decisions. If there are mistakes, let them be your own mistakes so that you can learn from them, not someone else's mistakes, from which you will learn nothing except, perhaps, why you should have made the decisions yourself in the first place!

> No matter how many advisers you have or how much counsel you seek from experts, the decision is yours to make, and only you are responsible for that decision. Be sure that the final decision is always yours.

USING OTHER SPECIALISTS' SERVICES

You may occasionally need the help of other technical and professional specialists, but you need also to know when and how to use their services wisely and in such a way that they serve your best interests and preserve your control. (More on this in Chapter 5.) Of course, the opposite is true, too: Other independent consultants may call on you for help in developing their own practices or for collaboration on projects.

Collaborations

The point was made earlier (and will be elaborated on at length later, in Chapter 9) that in the feast and famine business of consulting, it is always a quandary for you when you are in a feast mode and have more business than you can handle. The immediate choices are to hire help or turn the business away, neither one a desirable choice normally. However, there are several other choices possible: You can call on another consultant to collaborate or help in some other way—as a subcontractor, as an associate, or as a consultant.

This is a resource that can work both ways. You can turn to other consultants for help in periods of excessive demand, and you can reinforce your own marketing by making yourself available to collaborate with or support other consultants when they are overloaded. Moreover, you can do this on the basis of charging each other a discounted rate or simply referring the work to another, with mutual agreement that the other will refer work to you, as appropriate.

As part of your marketing program, then, you may want to seek out other consultants via membership in a consultants association and enter into working agreements that will benefit both of you.

> Consider setting up agreements with other consultants to refer work to each other, either as mutual courtesy or at special, discounted fees.

There is another aspect to this idea of referring projects to other consultants. It is setting up a web of

virtual corporation group of independent consultants who agree to work cooperatively on projects requiring teams of consultants with various specialties.

such agreements to create what has come to be called a *virtual corporation* by those who have organized such an entity.

The Virtual Corporation

A virtual corporation is a group of independent consultants who have agreed that they will collaborate with or otherwise support each other to be able to accept and satisfy requirements for larger projects than any can or would want to try to handle alone, or for projects requiring several different specialties. These would be projects calling for a number of kinds of consultants, so that several of those who are members of the cooperative or group of consultants would work together under the leadership of whoever brought in the contract or, more likely, the lead. There would, of course, be some standard operating system agreed to earlier, and if the lead called for a proposal, writing that would be a cooperative effort, too.

Such an arrangement could be made to work well only if the rules of running it were not too time-consuming nor so burdensome as to interfere with the individual consultants' normal work. The advance planning and agreement on the operating rules of the virtual corporation must therefore be flexible enough not to defeat one's purpose in becoming an independent consultant in the first place. You would have to decide just how much independence you would want to give up to make the virtual corporation idea work. The more practical idea is simply to form a rather loose association in which all agree to work cooperatively in a referral or discounted fee program as their schedules permit. That would allow the spontaneous formation of a group banded together for a project, a proposal, or any other joint effort. (That, incidentally, is in keeping with a modern idea in government procurement, in which the government favors having two or more companies team together to handle major contracts.)

Independent consultants can band together to form a virtual corporation or a loose association of cooperating independent consultants in a mutual referral program.

Finding Associates

To enable the virtual corporation or even a loose association of independent consultants, you will need to have ready access to a large roster of other consultants who have agreed to be part of the arrangement. Mutual membership in a large association of independent consultants is the most convenient way to find other consultants willing to participate, and it may even be possible to arrange to have the association sponsor the program.

All this activity of mutual referrals of projects to co-operating consulting associates and of such programs as virtual corporations is a good adjunct to your main marketing programs, and perhaps especially useful in helping you get your practice started, but it should not distract you from regular marketing. Marketing must be a serious business and carried out faithfully.

One way that should work efficiently and not burden anyone greatly is to set up an e-mail discussion group of consultants agreeing to work as part of a virtual corporation. The e-mail group would be the exchange medium and the announcement medium when one needs help and wants to announce the opportunity, describe what is needed, and call for responses.

MARKETING

Marketing is not just a system or process, nor a mechanical program in any sense. It is both method and art, and it is probably the most important function of your business. (Later, in Chapter 6, we'll get into the detail and depth of coverage the subject merits.) You should have a structured program, although it is typical of one-person enterprises to fly by the seat of one's pants—that is, make up the program and the rules as you go along, reacting spontaneously to daily experiences and learning. That is one of the major advantages of smallness: It is viable for such an enterprise to make changes and adjustments almost continuously because, as an individual, you can make instant decisions, adapt to conditions of the moment, modify policy, and change directions abruptly, which the larger organization usually cannot do. Still, it is certainly advisable to have at least a general marketing plan and program, with a clear goal and some itinerary of activities you hope will lead to the goal.

Regardless of how much or how little you have planned marketing at the outset, be sure that you fully understand its importance. Marketing is not something you can or should delegate. You may find it useful to seek help from others, but marketing is something on which you should have firm rein personally; it is that important.

> Nothing is more critical to your success than the quality and consistency of your marketing efforts. There is never a time when it is unnecessary to market or you are too busy to market—to seek new clients. Neglecting your marketing is a first step toward failure.

operating capital
money needed for day-to-day expenses and operating costs.

OPERATING CAPITAL

Operating capital is another matter of critical importance, one to be examined more closely in the next chapter but that merits a few words here. In an informal private survey I conducted of consultants' opinions on the most important considerations in starting a practice, many said that it is advisable (some said "necessary") to have enough capital to support yourself and your business for a year—that is, to subsidize your business with personal funds on the assumption that it will take at least a year for your new practice to become self-supporting. Unfortunately, few independent consultants have that much of a cash reserve when they start, and so they must market energetically, aggressively, and unceasingly, in the beginning at least. (Those who are able may start with a part-time independent consulting practice, but that is usually rather difficult to manage.) Marketing, plus practicing rigorous cost avoidance, will help you survive that first year or two while you are building a practice, even if you are not well funded. So conserve whatever capital you have or can manage to acquire.

Make do with what you already have—an outdated computer and printer that you can still manage to use to satisfy your needs. Don't have fancy stationery printed. There are several excellent computer programs that will turn out nice letterheads for you. (I still print all my own stationery, labels, forms, and similar items.) If you don't have some old furniture at home that you can use in your new office, you can find good used office furniture in excellent condition for a fraction of what it would cost you new. Shop around for the best prices. I have often found vendors that have simple listings in the Yellow Pages to offer goods and services at much lower prices than those that run the large advertisements. These are sound business practices.

> The question of finances is always an important one, of course, but it need not be an insoluble problem for most independent consultants. Careful planning (preferably as part of your business plan) and conservative policies can minimize financial needs.

A BUSINESS PLAN

The matter of a business plan has become a subject of wide interest in recent years. There have been a number of books written on the subject, and there are today a few business plan consultants who specialize in helping business organizations write their business plans.

> A business plan is a detailed road map for your business, including plans for start-up, management, finances, and—especially—marketing. Time invested in developing a thorough business plan is time well invested.

Most often, "business plan" is a euphemism for "loan proposal." That is, entrepreneurs write a business plan to persuade a bank to grant a loan or a venture capitalist to make an investment. You thus will find that most of the many books purporting to teach the reader how to write a business plan are focused principally on writing that kind of business plan—one intended to support a quest for financing by demonstrating the worthiness of the writer as a borrower or investment for the future. The business plan thus described, therefore, focuses on explaining in detail what the business will be and why it will be successful and a good risk for loans or investment. Achieving the latter effect is the main objective of the business proposal written to attract capital for either debt financing (borrowing money) or equity financing (attracting investors with risk capital).

Do not interpret this to mean that if your proposed venture is not seeking an injection of capital, you need not write a business plan; that is not true. Writing a business plan is always a good idea. A well-thought-out business plan is a carefully detailed business road map with a complete itinerary. It sets out your objectives and your planned routes for reaching them. Even if you do not require *investment capital*, as most independent consultants do not, the business plan is a valuable asset as a set of thought-out objectives and a road map for reaching them. Here is a trimmed-down outline of a business plan suitable for a small consulting practice. Don't hesitate to add to the outline shown here, for it should be fleshed out in terms of your own needs, with emphasis on marketing plans and including details of services to be offered.

investment capital
money used or required to start the business.

The Bobtailed Business Plan Outline

1. Mission statement:
   - ✔ Business you are in (key words to identify).
   - ✔ Essence of your business strategy (instant service, low cost, other).

2. Start-up capital requirement (estimate).

3. Start-up decisions:
   - ✔ Where office will be located (home, office building, other).
   - ✔ Starting fixtures, furniture, equipment, and supplies required.
   - ✔ Specific services to be offered to clients.
   - ✔ Short- and long-term goals and objectives, (size, capability, sales volume)

4. Marketing plan:
   - ✔ Profile of typical clients/prospective clients.
   - ✔ Competition anticipated, kind and number (suggestions for analyzing).
   - ✔ Advertising requirements and costs (full analysis).
   - ✔ Promotions planned and costs (full analysis).

5. Rate structure:
   - ✔ Basis (daily, hourly, fixed price, etc.).
   - ✔ Rates (discussions and suggestions).

6. Potential for diversification/other profit centers:

✔ Related services (examples and suggestions).

✔ Products (examples and suggestions).

7. Contingency plans:

✔ Alternative services/products, if and as necessary (suggestions).

✔ Alternative markets, if and as necessary (extended discussion).

8. Income projections (suggested analytical methods).

Although most business plans are written to be used as or in support of loan proposals, a well-written and well-thought-out business plan has great value as a guide to efficient operations, especially to marketing activity. You should have drafted a business plan even if you are not in quest of financing of any sort.

> Preparing even a simple business plan to set your thoughts down is worth doing, even if you are not seeking financing.

A note about business plans: Whether formal or informal, lengthy or brief, your business plan is not etched in stone. It is always tentative, in that it is a set of objectives based on your best estimates. That is the key: Estimates are your best guesses, based on whatever information is available and what you believe you can achieve. They are rarely exactly right. Remember that, and use your experience to revise and upgrade those estimates. Correct them to correspond more closely with what your experience now tells you are the facts. That is, review your business plan at regular intervals or when some event prompts you to take a good look at those earlier estimates. Update the business plan periodically so that it reflects your experience, the facts as you have learned them, so that your business plan is an ever more accurate, more reliable, and more valuable business tool. To do that most conveniently, your business plan should be a file (or perhaps a growing set of files) in your computer, possibly with a spreadsheet and database, so that you can easily and conveniently revise it and print out the latest version to post where it will be a constant reminder that you are not flying blind, but have a guide always at hand. Refer to it frequently to gauge your progress against the objectives you set for yourself earlier.

> Your business plan is not immutable. Far from it—it is never finished, for you should review and revise it regularly, probably at six-month intervals, to bring it up to date and correct any estimates that have proved inaccurate. Thus, the business plan steadily becomes more valuable.

COMMON WORK-AT-HOME PROBLEMS

There are problems in working at home, some of them common to home workers and dependent on what kinds of working conditions are most often encountered. For example, as a consultant, you may spend most of your time working on a client's premises, in the field, in your own office, or at some mix of these. You may start each day about the same way, or each day may be new and different. That depends on the kinds of contracts you sign, the kinds of services you specialize in, and perhaps other factors, such as your morning routine, which we will discuss shortly. The problems can be psychological, legal, or practical. Those I describe here thus may or may not apply to you individually.

Most of us who have an office at home and work there are envied by many of those who must travel to their own places of work every morning. They seem not to understand that there are problems with an office at home, too. There is rarely as much space as you would like to have, and there is little privacy, to name two immediate ones. You don't get the welcome break of lunch hour in your day when you go out with others from your office or meet a friend at some nearby eatery. Family members find it difficult to accept that your office door is closed, figuratively at least, during business hours. My own wife is a habitual offender, but even she leaves my office quietly when I scowl at her fiercely enough. Merely keeping regular hours in your office at home can become a problem if there is a single other person there with you during your office hours.

It is not only family members who threaten interruptions. Tradesmen and salespeople come knocking on your door. One consultant reports that she is fortunate enough to have a window that overlooks the front of her house so she can see who is knocking and decide whether to answer. But another home worker complained recently that he has many retired people as his neighbors, and they seem to be constantly knocking on his front door and interrupting his work. He asked an *Internet* discussion group for suggestions and got a number of predictable ones: Don't answer the door, post an explanation on the door, send letters to the neighbors, and post a Do Not Disturb sign. The best response suggested the wording of the sign:

 Internet like cyberspace, that world of electronic communications and business transactions.

> Do not disturb unless:
>
> **A:** The building is on fire.
>
> **B:** You have money for me.
>
> **C:** Elvis has been spotted in the building.

Another suggestion was an intercom with a front door microphone and speaker, or a more expensive system that would include a closed-circuit TV camera and monitor.

Working at home is not an unmixed blessing: It usually involves the problem of privacy and freedom to concentrate on your work. You may have to take specific measures to block out and prevent the disturbances that otherwise interrupt your work.

KEEPING OFFICE HOURS IN YOUR HOME

Among the most common obstacles to working at home is the psychological one, a fear that you will be unable to work at home because of distraction by the intrusions of your family or be unable to discipline yourself to keep office hours in your own home. It is one of the most common fears and one I experienced myself in the days before I first tried working in my own home. Probably most of my anticipatory fear was the result of warnings and predictions by others that I would have such problems. Most of those predictions seem to come from individuals who are employed on a job somewhere, and so I suspect they are motivated by an unconscious envy of those who are going to enjoy the freedom of self-employment in their own homes. In any case, try to resist anticipatory fears, no matter where or how the stimulus for such fear originates. Cross bridges when you come to them. If a problem arises out of your new working conditions, you will have to solve it, and you need faith in yourself and your ability to do so.

Many people are conditioned by long practice to feel that they must have someplace to *go to* every morning. It is a psychological need. They need to have that feeling of going off to work if they are to have a suitable attitude—be conditioned to work—for the day. They believe that they must be surrounded by what they have learned to regard as a business or working environment and that they cannot discipline themselves to attend strictly to business all day long in what is to them not a working environment because it is so close to the refrigerator and TV.

It is a real enough problem, but it can be and is being solved by many people obviously, since the work-at-home population is growing rapidly. The solutions are many and varied, according to the individual circumstances, which are themselves highly variable. You may have to solve both psychological and practical problems to be able to discipline yourself and concentrate on work in the informal and relaxed atmosphere of your own home. Solutions vary as widely as do individual characteristics and needs. There is a related problem of productivity, another important matter that takes on special significance for the worker at home.

One way to solve this problem is to develop a new morning routine. (You no doubt have one already, probably an unconscious routine, suited to whatever you do now to earn a living.) In a short while, I developed a new morning routine, one suited to my new situation of going to work by entering an office next door to my bedroom. But before I do that every morning, I go through my new morning routine of getting my eyes and consciousness fully awake and alert so that I am ready for work.

First is a trip to the kitchen and my morning cup of coffee, with the morning newspaper. The coffee helps me wake up. After reading those sections of the newspaper that interest me, my eyes can begin to focus properly again, and I do the crossword puzzle. That gets my brain warmed up and in gear. (That takes about as much time as I would otherwise spend gulping down my morning coffee, getting dressed, and driving to my office somewhere at the other end of a series of stressful traffic stops and rude other commuters.) By then I am fully awake, alert, and ready for work, although not dressed to leave the house. (I spend large parts of the day at my work in pajamas.) I am now conditioned to enter that totally different world of my office and start immediately to work. But even then I have what is an important routine to me: I review what I did yesterday—evaluating, editing, and revising. Then I am project conditioned—thinking in terms of whatever my current project involves so I can pick up where I finished the day before and go on with a seamless continuity.

It should not take long before you have developed your own morning routine. By then, working at home will seem to you to be the most natural state of affairs imaginable.

> In a short while, you will develop your own morning routine, replacing whatever routine you had previously. That will help you adapt to working at home comfortably.

THE NEED FOR A WORKING ENVIRONMENT

If you have trouble feeling that you are "at work" in your office at home, endeavor to create what seems to you to be a true working environment. Try first to analyze what you sense is a working environment, for that varies widely. There are some people who can work at the kitchen table or set up two orange crates as a desk and chair in a musty basement and work cheerfully all day there, completely shutting out noisy children, tradesmen knocking at the door, clattering garbage cans being emptied outside, and all the other normal noises and distractions of everyday life. (One of my own former employers, today the owner of an international billion-dollar business headquartered on New York's Park Avenue, actually did launch that enterprise years ago at his mother's kitchen table!) These are exceptional individuals; not too many of us can attain quite that degree of self-sufficient concentration and discipline. But even accepting our limitations in that respect, some of us go to extremes in our negative approach to the potential problem, working overtime at conditioning ourselves to make our fears a reality.

Your attitude can itself be cause or cure. If you firmly expect to have trouble disciplining yourself to work at home all day, it represents programming yourself and it may easily become a self-fulfilling prophecy. You can persuade yourself to make the prophecy or fear a reality. But you can also take the opposite approach: Condition yourself to believe that you can and will work comfortably and steadily in your office at home. If necessary, take out five or ten minutes each day to lie down quietly and meditate. View yourself working quietly and energetically at whatever you normally do in your work. Have a session like that twice a day for a week or two, then once a day for another week or two, and then occasionally as a refresher. That alone will be helpful and probably will be all you need to develop a healthful, positive attitude.

There are other things you can do that will help you learn to regard an office at home as a workplace just as much as you do an office in an employer's facilities many miles away: You can create a working environment in your home office. Most of us need to have our own special space, comfortable furnishings, and a reasonable measure of privacy or isolation. To work at home, you probably need to establish a working atmosphere, such as a room that is furnished as an office is normally furnished, with a conventional desk and chair, telephone, typewriter, computer, and whatever else is needed for the everyday conduct of your business.

In my own case, I created an office that matches my sense of what feels like a working environment to me. I converted a bedroom to an office by installing office furniture and equipment: a proper desk, an office chair, bookshelves, a filing cabinet, a bulletin board, my computer, printer, copier, wall clock, and all the other trappings that are like those in offices I occupied in office buildings for years. When I close the door, I am in my office and all is well with the world.

> For many, the solution to the psychological problems of working at home is to create a work environment by fitting the home office out with the physical trappings of a conventional office and shutting out all else from nine to five or whatever your working hours are.

That is the first step in solving the problem of working at home: Create a separate world that is not part of your residence, despite being located physically within it, setting it up in a manner that is appropriate to whatever your needs are so you can feel that you are truly at work. Whether you bundle up on a cold day and get your automobile out to drive off to somewhere or stroll a few steps down the hall to your office should make no difference. Once there, you are at work. Close the door, if necessary, and even post a Busy—Do Not Disturb sign on your door, if that helps, but do condition your thinking to accept that this is your place of work, another world. Your home and your personal affairs are *outside* this room, and they should be kept outside, as your work is kept inside.

Keep regular hours. If possible, adjust your hours to your conditions. If you are an early riser, early morning hours may be your most productive time. (I usually have several hours of work done before I shower and dress every morning.) Or you may find it advantageous to put in a few hours late at night, when things have settled down and it is, indeed, quiet. But make it your business to establish a regimen that works for you and you can live with; then stick to it. You need to have a firm commitment to a routine and a regular schedule, at least in the beginning.

Sometimes your family—children, spouse, or others—can be a problem of a different kind: Family members may have trouble understanding your need to keep regular hours, undisturbed and uninterrupted, that you are at work just as much as when you go off to an employer's offices. They tend to feel free to burst in on you at any time to ask a question or demand that you fix a leaky faucet, prepare lunch, join them in watching a TV show, or drive them somewhere. Tell them that you are not at home. You are at work, and you will talk to them when work is over and you are at home again.

Getting privacy and respect by all for your needed privacy when you are working is a difficult problem, but it is amenable to solution. If your spouse or others go off to a job every morning and/or your children are in school every day, you have at least several hours a day when you have the house or apartment all to yourself. But if you have a spouse at home, you may have the kind of problem cited and have to look for a solution. And one direct way to solve the problem of interruptions by a spouse is sometimes fairly easy to solve by the simple expedient of making your spouse your business partner! Make sure that he or she has as much stake in the business and as much to say about the conduct of the business as you do. You may soon find yourself driven harder by your spouse/business partner than you ever were by the most demanding employer.

> Making your spouse your business partner is often the best way to create a work environment at home. Spouses may eclipse you in working efforts when brought into the business.

WORKAHOLISM

A frequent complaint by work-at-homes is burnout. They complain that they are just weary of so many hours and so much hard work. But that is because they are driving themselves excessively. They have become workaholics, hardly having a life outside their offices and businesses. And it is true that they are burning themselves out by failing to take enough time off to live, as well as to work—for weekends, holidays, and vacations.

There are two common reasons for this kind of lapse into excessive dedication to the home business: low profit and inability to say no.

In many cases, the individual is not turning enough gross profit to draw a decent salary due to excessively low prices. You must guard against the temptation to deceive yourself that you are "just doing this to get started," and you will raise your prices later. Unfortunately, your business may never last until "later," and so you may never get to raise your prices! Moreover, you don't want a reputation for being the cheapest in town. That is a negative image for a consultant. But this is not all—in fact, this situation is related to a much larger and more common problem that leads to workaholism and consequent business difficulties.

Many fledgling entrepreneurs who are underfinanced to begin with (a most common situation) become so conditioned to the desperate need for sales and money that they are unable to say no to any business offered and to any demand made by a client. And so they undertake many impossible tasks and accept many sales that they should have refused or only accepted with agreement to a much larger fee.

That is a major problem of entrepreneurship. To be a successful entrepreneur you must learn how to say no to some business, to business that is not worth having—that is, to business that is really outside the normal bounds of whatever you sell or do. You must learn to say no to all business that you must make special price cuts to get. You must learn to say no to all business that is conditional on your meeting unreasonable demands, such as impossible delivery dates. (There are exceptions, but they ought to be most definitely exceptions.)

The cause of workaholism is not necessarily enthusiasm. It may be the result of shortcomings in business management, making you work overtime to compensate. Be suspicious of such problems if you find yourself working more than ordinary hours.

LEARN TO SAY NO (AND HOW TO SAY IT)

A strange thing happens when you begin saying no to customers who demand impossible prices and performance, if you know how to say no: They usually become far more tractable and reasonable. That has been my experience, and many others have verified that it is a truism. It takes a bit of fortitude to say no to business, but then no one says success comes easily.

I am one who has trouble refusing business, and so I had to work at learning how to say no without rancor, sadly, as a necessary duty. The first time that I can recall forcing myself to do so I was reacting to a client who always—almost automatically—objected to my price, my schedule, and anything else he could find as something about which to carp. Since I patiently allowed him to do this, he extended this to demands for revision, changing things as he got new ideas, all without extra compensation, of course.

He was a pleasant enough fellow, rather likable, as such clients often are. When I finally could not endure more of his business, I refused a new assignment he brought me with these words, spoken quietly:

"Mr. Smith, I am truly sorry to say this, but I can't accept any more work from you."

He looked surprised and asked, "Why not?"

"You are just too demanding, Mr. Smith. You quibble over price, and over everything else, demand much more work than you have a right to expect from me, and make me fear that I am about to have a heart attack. Let's remain friends. I will say hello to you when we meet on the street, and I will be happy to buy you a friendly drink anytime, but I can't do business with you."

Smith withdrew, looking puzzled and hurt, but he was back within hours, apologizing to me for any problems of the past, pleading with me to help him get this newest piece of work done, and promising faithfully never again to give me any trouble.

I took him back as a client and, true to his word,

never again had any problems with him. He became one of my best clients.

I was surprised, of course, but I learned from this that it was the only way to respond to most troublesome clients, and that the results were usually the same: The client begged to be taken back and promised to be a model client ever after.

To do this well, be careful to exhibit regret, not anger or rebellion at being forced to turn away the client's work. Explain why you are doing so as tactfully as you can, making it clear that it is a totally impersonal reaction and just a business decision that you are forced to make. If the client never returns, you haven't lost much, of course; but you will often be surprised by the kind of results described here. The client has had a shock: rejection, an unusual act by a supplier. That seems to teach the client respect for you and your work. (Rejecting a client is interpreted by the client as a demand for respect.)

> Getting rid of a troublesome client is surprisingly difficult, but trying to do so may convert the troublesome client into a highly desirable one.

IT CAN BE A LONELY JOB

Some people are loners by choice and actually prefer solitude as a steady diet, whereas most of us probably choose the solitary environment only occasionally, as a relief. We normally prefer to be in the company of others during business hours. But there are also those who absolutely require the comfort and reassurance of being with others, having face-to-face contact. They find working alone, with only occasional contact with others, intolerable.

Your own work may be such that you leave your office frequently (perhaps every day) to meet or work with clients and others, so that you do not spend a great part of your working day in solitude. Or you may be on the telephone a great deal as part of your business activity, and that is a counter for solitude as well. Loneliness is not, then, a problem for you. On the other hand, many work-at-home businesses are essentially lonely jobs, and the long silences of the day can be quite depressing. If that is the case with you, and your business is one that keeps you working alone in your office all day, you will have to seek a solution. I long ago developed my own method for combating the basically lonely job of writing, and later found that a great many of my writer friends were doing the same thing: We all use e-mail discussion groups for breaks in the isolation.

I use a modem and dedicated telephone line with my computer, and through that I maintain a steady correspondence with others, taking breaks occasionally to read and respond to the message traffic on the electronic discussion groups of the Internet. I also find that while I use it as a needed break from the typical solitude of full-time writing, I also am able to turn this channel of communication into a useful business asset. Consultants can get much of their business, directly and indirectly, from their e-mail friends and contacts.

Another approach to interrupting unwanted solitude is to make it your business to get out of the office and the house at least once or twice a day, even if it is just running an errand to buy a new printer cassette or a trip to a favorite local restaurant for lunch. Better yet, meet a friend or business acquaintance for lunch occasionally. Or take your spouse to lunch if you can pry him or her away from his or her own computer.

Of course, there are exceptions. While some people require absolute silence when they work, finding it difficult to concentrate otherwise, others prefer soft music in the background, and anyone who has ever worked in the city room of a large newspaper has probably observed that there are individuals who actually enjoy working in the midst of bedlam. If you are one of those, you might enjoy playing an office-sounds tape all day, providing a soft background of typing, chatter, and other typical sounds of a busy office. (Such tapes are available commercially, although their intended use is as window dressing—to provide the illusion of a busy office when the work-at-home entrepreneur is talking to customers and prospective customers on the telephone.)

> Extended solitude and loneliness are problems for some who work at home, but they can be combated through use of e-mail and deliberate breaks in your daily routine.

PRODUCTIVITY

Aside from the psychological and practical problems of working at home, there is the corollary problem of productivity. Will you be more or less productive working in your office at home than you were working for someone else?

Many people working in large organizations are convinced that much of their time each day is wasted. They waste time traveling to and from their places of work every day. They waste time with innumerable distractions, most of them unnecessary, every day. They waste time with inefficient standard processes and procedures dictated by the bureaucracies for which they work. They would be far more productive if they worked away from all of this and in an environment where they were in complete control. So they believe. But is it so?

The temptation to be the most lenient employer in the world is sometimes overpowering when you are your own boss. Typical accounts by freelance writers, whose work is inherently solitary and self-imposed, illustrate the point. They recount the incessant pencil sharpening, straightening papers on the desk, repeated trips to the kitchen for another cup of coffee, cleaning out already orderly desk drawers, staring out the window, and innumerable other evasions every morning to avoid facing the day's work tasks, especially that most difficult one of getting new ideas and solving work-related problems that caused you to quit work a little early yesterday because you were too tired and worn out to tackle the problem at the end of a long day. Incidentally, you can get a lot of help with these problems by belonging to and being active in those relevant e-mail discussion groups we talked about in the previous section. I air my problems in the groups to which I belong, and I get assistance quite often, sometimes as specific directions for solving certain computer problems, writing problems, and business problems.

Some of that is peculiar to the nature of freelance writing and other creative work. For many of us, the mental pump must be primed every morning, and many writers have no convenient and reliable way of doing it. Each morning is a struggle to somehow trigger the beginning of the day's flow of thoughts. But much of it simply reflects difficulty in imposing the sentence of work on oneself every morning. It is not peculiar to freelance writers, but a problem or potential problem for every self-employed individual to some extent, but especially the work-at-home, with so many temptations to interrupt work and its difficulties.

Beware of being too good to yourself as your own employer. Try to remember at all times that your business pays you as an employee who is expected to work as hard as any other employee. Try to think of the business as the employer, a separate entity.

Now you have been through a fairly lengthy general review of what working at home means to most of us who do so every day. From here on, we are going to get at these various areas discussed briefly in this chapter, examining them in much greater detail. We shall also have a look at other subjects that have so far not been raised.

Chapter

2

Capital and Cash Flow Management

Money is always a serious matter, and it includes all aspects of financing the new business and managing its cash flow.

FRONT-END PROBLEMS

There are many problems in business, but two that must have your attention quite early in the process of setting up your venture concern money—the two kinds of front-end financing needed. There is capital needed for start-up—for purchasing equipment, supplies, furniture, and whatever else is necessary to get ready to do business, to get the door open. But there is also the need for operating capital for the months until the business begins to produce enough income to stand on its own feet and pay its daily bills. It is possible, of course, that you may be fortunate enough to start with clients who pay promptly and even clients who pay generous *retainers* easily, but it is more likely that yours will be the typical case of *cash flow* problems.

 retainer
nonreturnable fee or advance deposit to start consultant doing work called for.

 cash flow
the continuous availability of cash, as distinct from receivables.

51

Be prepared to face the problem of being cash poor in the beginning, even if you win clients and contracts immediately. It is reassuring to have accounts receivable, but the cash due you on those accounts can be agonizingly slow in coming.

CASH FLOW MANAGEMENT

A great many individuals get brilliant ideas for business ventures and are then stymied by lack of capital. Many businesses are stillborn because of this problem; many others are launched despite the problem of insufficient capital, but ultimately perish because of that lack of financial depth. It is essential that you have a little money of your own, even if you enjoy A1 credit and plan to borrow. Banks are notoriously unwilling to provide 100 percent financing. They usually want the assurance that you are undertaking personal risk. Fortunately, consulting does not usually require a large front-end investment, but it may well be that you will have to raise considerably more start-up capital than you yourself can provide. In that case, you will need a business plan, as described in the previous chapter. Let us assume here, however, that like most independent consultants, you can manage to provide enough of your own capital to get started on a modest scale, but only by being cautious and conservative in your spending, improvising fixtures and furniture, using what you already have, and practicing extreme frugality in other ways. Even then, you may soon find that you do not have enough operating capital to pay daily expenses and draw even a modest salary while the business is growing slowly.

That's a problem of *cash flow management*, and yet it is a separate problem common to start-ups. Many beginners in business know that they must have at least a little investment capital to start doing business on even a modest scale, but they often do not recognize the need for operating capital. They assume, naively, that income will

cash flow management the methods and procedures used to establish and maintain the availability of ready cash for normal operating expenses.

begin to flow as soon as they open their doors and win a client or two. Alas, they soon discover two factors they had not counted on:

First, business does not usually start with a great rush. Most often, business and income grow slowly and take a long time before showing enough profit to take care of daily expenses. And that is especially true for a home-based venture, which is often home-based of necessity because of a shortage of capital.

Second, even when business is good and grows rapidly, collections, as they used to refer to what is now called cash flow, are often slow. That is, in many businesses much of the sales volume is with customers who maintain open accounts (charges) and who will probably not pay their bills for 30 days or more. (Even large organizations that, presumably, can easily afford to pay their bills on time, often deliberately "age" their *payables* to benefit their own cash flow, and may thus take as long as 60 to 90 days to pay you.) Before long, you can have a great deal of money "on the street"—owed to you and on your ledger as *receivables*—so that even though you are doing a satisfactory volume of business, you are being choked by the lack of cash flowing in, while the bills continue to mount.

 payable bill received or money due someone, listed on books but not yet paid.

As a result, unless you are fortunate enough to be especially well financed in the beginning, still hold down a job, or have some other source of income, you will have to practice strict economies and even subsidize your own practice in other ways, such as keeping the cash you draw for personal use to an absolute minimum until you start to get an adequate flow of income from your practice.

 receivable money due and listed on books but not yet received.

> Be prepared to go with the smallest possible personal draw or salary at first, and practice the strictest economies in the beginning to give your new business the maximum chance for survival and success, even if your marketing enables you to build a clientele rapidly.

Ironically, this is especially difficult for the young business with rapidly growing sales. Suppose that you do $5,000 in sales the first month. By the end of the second month, we will assume, you have collected that $5,000 and have the gross profit on that in the bank. But you do $6,500 of business the second month, so that original $5,000 has long since gone into the inventory and other expenses incurred in doing more business. And that process can continue for some time, the cost of doing more business growing more rapidly than the cash flow (collections). Even for the well-financed new business, the pinch of the cash flow problem can reach crisis proportions in the first year.

It is because of this, among other typical problems, that you must expect it to take at least a year or two for your new business to begin to earn a net profit. In fact, venture capitalists looking at potential investments in new businesses tend to study them on the basis of whether they are likely to become profitable in three to four years.

> Winning a lot of business immediately upon opening your doors may be a mixed blessing because you must finance your work to attend to all that business until you can bill the clients and collect for it. You must take direct steps to manage your cash flow.

MANAGING YOUR CASH FLOW

Cost reduction is a worthy activity in any business, new or well established. Cost avoidance is even better than cost reduction, however. That means never having excess and unnecessary spending—that is, not buying anything you really do not need while you are struggling to establish your new business.

As critics say to hopeful young singers and comics

auditioning for their first shot at show biz, don't quit your day job. Not if you can help it. If at all possible, run your new home-based venture on a part-time basis and don't draw a salary. Put every dollar of profit back into the business to help it grow.

The typical mistakes that you can make are understandable. Like so many others, you start out flushed with enthusiasm for your can't miss idea for an independent venture and buoyed by encouragement from friends and relatives. Self-assured and confident, you start out in great style, with handsome new furniture, shiny new equipment, expensive stationery and other office supplies, and a generous advertising budget.

Of course, almost all of that expense is not absolutely necessary, except, perhaps, the advertising. You can do as much business at a second-hand desk or even a kitchen table as you can at a new $1,200 solid-oak desk and president's chair. (Recall the billion-dollar company that the owner started at his mother's kitchen table and which now is headquartered on New York's Park Avenue.) Expensive stationery does not produce a penny's worth of business that more modest stationery would not have produced. (Imagine how many tons of expensive stationery wind up being used as scratch pads.) And expensive copiers and other shiny new office machines often wind up gathering dust in closets.

You can't really anticipate with complete accuracy what you will need. I once had a regular and substantial copying expense, taking my typewriter-prepared manuscripts to a local copy shop almost daily. I was tempted to invest as much as $3,000 in my own copier. I resisted the temptation, fortunately, for not too much later I bought my first computer and word processing system. From that time on, I have had only occasional need for copying, and rarely for more than a single sheet or two—which are provided by my little fax machine now as an incidental convenience. On the other hand, I was entirely mistaken about how useful a computer would be to me; to my surprise, it became absolutely indispensable. I would be benefiting today if I had bought a system earlier, for I would then have more of my manuscripts on computer disks. However, when I did buy my first computer, I investigated the field quite thoroughly before deciding what was most suitable for my needs.

The lesson here is to think carefully before making investments. Having copies made at a local copy shop was a business expense. Buying a copier would have been a substantial investment, one I would have come to regret as unnecessary after a few months. Sometimes it is better to own things, but often it is better to rent. Think carefully before making new investments.

> When your business needs something, there are usually three choices: Buy new, buy secondhand, or rent. Think carefully about which is the best choice for meeting your needs while conserving your cash.

Understanding the nature of your business helps you plan methods for maximizing your cash flow. Most businesses require either heavy initial investment capital in inventory and/or equipment or heavy operating capital for labor.

LABOR-INTENSIVE VERSUS CAPITAL-INTENSIVE REQUIREMENTS

Most business ventures require an investment of some sort, if only to equip an office. However, investment does not necessarily mean cash. It can mean supplying any asset you own personally to your business. That could be furniture, a computer, an automobile, or other property. Interestingly enough, if you use your personal automobile for business and charge your business a per-mile figure, that falls into the category of renting; if you choose to sell your automobile to your business, that puts it into the investment capital category.

Thus, there are many businesses that can be launched with very little cash up front. In terms of kinds of costs, most business ventures are either *labor-intensive* or *capital-intensive*. These are terms that refer to the major costs in capitalization and operating expenses. What that means, in simple terms, is that the business is based on selling either labor or products. In a services business that relies primarily on one's experience, know-how, and judgment, as in the case of independent consulting, the chief cost is labor. Thus such a business is labor-intensive. A business selling a product requires an inventory, warehousing, and other investment in *capital items*, and is therefore a capital-intensive business.

All businesses have overhead expenses, the expenses for keeping your door open—rent, heat, light, insurance, and similar costs. In an independent consulting business, you bill clients for your labor in their behalf, and your objective is to be able to bill as much of your time as possible, for your idle time is overhead. There is nowhere else to charge your idle time except to your own overhead. It is characteristic of labor-intensive businesses that idle time of service providers must be kept to an absolute minimum. (That will become a little clearer when we discuss that area of your business—costs and fees—in Chapter 4, so we will not dwell on it here.)

 labor-intensive business activity selling direct labor as a major commodity and cost item.

 capital-intensive business operations dependent primarily on capital investment and availability.

 capital item an item, usually one with relatively long life, costing more than a figure set arbitrarily by the business owner as the defining point for all capital items.

> Overhead is the enemy of success in business, and idle time is a prime source of excessive overhead in independent consulting, so you must always take steps to minimize idle time.

SOLVING FINANCIAL PROBLEMS

Financial problems do not solve themselves, of course, and borrowing money is often more an expedient than a solution. In fact, it is a good idea to make borrowing a last resort. The imaginative entrepreneur often comes up with ingenious ideas for solving business problems, including financial problems. One of the ways is to have your clients finance you or, at least, help you with the financing of your operations.

DEPOSITS, RETAINERS, AND PROGRESS PAYMENTS

In many businesses, with the use of the creative imagination every independent consultant ought to have, you can use the customer's money, paid in advance, to fill the order.

One of my own successes in getting customer financing was an announcement of a book I was in the process of writing. I invited readers of a popular newsletter to send in orders, with advance payment, but cautioned that they would have to wait about 90 days. However, in return for paying in advance and waiting, they were guaranteed immediate shipment of the first copies off the press, plus a bonus, which I did not define then. (I did not know then what it was to be, but after deciding to publish a newsletter I gave those first buyers free subscriptions.) Enough orders, with advance payment, arrived to finance the printing and shipping of the books and the new newsletter! That demonstrates what can be done with a bit of imagination.

In any custom work, such as consulting, there is the built-in hazard that what you are doing has no value to anyone but the specific client for whom you are doing it. Even if the work results in a product of some sort, as in the case of design work, the product has no application elsewhere, hence no alternative value. If the client fails to pay you, you have a 100 percent loss. Be aware of that possible hazard in undertaking custom work of any kind. The best insurance against loss is getting paid up front.

It is not always possible to get paid your entire fee up front for at least two reasons: Not every client is willing to pay the entire fee in advance, and in some arrangements you must charge by the hour or day without being certain how many hours or days will be required to complete the work. In all cases, however, you should arrange for retainers, deposits, and/or *progress payments*. If the work is to be long-term, you should get agreement to bill and be paid periodically, perhaps once a month or once every two weeks, with at least a first payment or retainer in advance. If the work is relatively short-term, a good plan is to get about one-third the estimated amount in advance as a deposit or retainer, another third at some predetermined midpoint (such as upon completion of a draft), and the final third upon completion or delivery of the work itself.

progress payments
partial payments of the entire fee, paid at stated points in the progress of the work.

There are always exceptions because there are always exceptional circumstances. If you are undertaking a task for a major organization whose ability and willingness to pay are beyond question, you may be willing to forgo advance payment. For a short-term assignment with a large organization, advance payment is sometimes impracticable because the job will be completed before the large organization can complete the paperwork and get a check drawn for a retainer. Even so, ask first for the retainer, if only to help your cash flow. Sometimes even the largest corporations have facilities to make on-the-spot payments of what are to them small amounts of money. Be sure, however, that there is firm commitment by the client for the work and for your retention for the work. A retainer or advance deposit is certain evidence of firm commitment, but it is always a good policy to have some form of written agreement or *purchase order*. There are enough horror stories to illustrate the soundness of that admonition, such as one related to me by consultant Steve W.

purchase order
an agreement that is normally an informal contract.

Steve works in the energy field, and was invited to handle an assignment for a large coal company in West Virginia. Accordingly, Steve drove for many hours from his home in Michigan to the offices of the client company. He had to wait awhile for Mr. X, who had retained him verbally by telephone. When Mr. X arrived and they sat down in his office, Steve stated that he was ready to go to work.

To his dismay, he was rebuffed by Mr. X, who now claimed he had not actually retained Steve but only discussed with him his availability for possible retention and assignment.

Steve realized at this point that he had been victimized by an employee who had acted without authority and was now denying his action, and so Steve had to return home empty-handed. (There was a happy ending because Steve took some wise action promptly, but that is beside the point here. In most cases of this kind, the consultant must bite the bullet and be consoled only with having learned an important lesson.)

I confess to having myself been a victim of similar circumstances more than once. I later learned to ask for a purchase order or at least a confirming letter, as well as a retainer, before doing anything. I found, over the years, that when I was able to get a retainer there never were problems in collecting my bill later. It was only in those cases where I crossed my fingers and gambled with an unknown, small organization that could not or would not pay a retainer that I sometimes suffered a loss. (Unfortunately, I learned, even a written contract with the client is no guarantee that you will not be victimized and suffer a loss.)

There is another way that clients can be persuaded to help you finance your operations: I found that in most cases when the assignment required travel I could preserve my own resources by requesting that the client furnish an airline ticket. If there is not time enough to have a ticket mailed to you, the client can always arrange to have a ticket waiting at the airline counter of your own airport or issued by a travel agency near your home. Too, clients can and often will arrange your hotel reservations and have your accommodations billed to their accounts.

These measures make good sense because otherwise you must tie up considerable cash of your own without profit to you and perhaps for 30 to 90 days. So far, I have never had difficulty in making these arrangements with an out-of-town client. In fact, on some occasions the client provided these services without being asked to, anticipating the need to do so as routine.

Many businesses are financed by their customers, although the customers may not realize that they are helping their suppliers. For example, many businesses operate on a cash-only basis, requiring payment when the order is placed. In fact, there are situations where the customer finances the entrepreneur by making payment months in advance of the delivery of the service.

The U.S. Postal Service, for example, is always paid in advance—often many months in advance—of providing the service. In fact, the Postal Service has many millions of dollars paid in advance and financing operations: Every stamp in your desk drawer, every dollar of credit in your postage meter, every dollar of deposit for bulk mail and permit mail is an advance to the Postal Service against services to be delivered when demanded, giving the Postal Service interest-free use of your money! But it is not only the Postal Service that is so smiled upon; there are many ventures in the private sector that are paid in advance, sometimes well in advance, of providing the services. Here are a few examples:

- ✔ Airlines and other transportation services get paid immediately in advance of providing their services at full list prices, but they also offer many special arrangements where they get paid well in advance of providing those services. They offer special rates during their off-peak hours but require reservations and payment—deposits, at least—well in advance.
- ✔ Delivery services allow open accounts for their regular customers, but those without open accounts pay in advance for delivery services.
- ✔ Travel bureaus and tour packages get paid—with deposits at least—well in advance.
- ✔ Most periodical subscriptions are paid in advance, as much as a year and sometimes several years in advance of their service.
- ✔ Advertising in periodicals and other media—radio and TV—is usually paid for in advance, often three or more months in advance for advertising space or time.

✔ Most mail order dealers are paid when the merchandise is ordered, even if it is not shipped for several weeks. (Under current law, a mail order dealer may take up to 30 days to fill the order.) When the customer uses a credit card to make the purchase, the customer does not have to pay immediately, but the seller gets his or her money immediately.

All of these give the entrepreneur interest-free use of the customer's money for some time, ranging from days to months. That is a significant business advantage, and one you may wish to consider in planning your business. (You can deposit credit card charges in your account and not have to wait for clearance, as you do when depositing checks.) But that is not yet all.

Some kinds of ventures are cash in advance by their nature. Mail order, direct mail, and subscriptions are among these. Many entities doing business in *cyberspace* (e.g., the Internet) get paid in advance, usually by credit card charges. Although there are some exceptions, normally all orders are paid for in advance by currency, check, money order, or credit card. Even when long-term advance payment is not the customary way to do business in some fields, you can sometimes contrive to do so with a little imagination.

cyberspace
the hypothetical space in which electronic communication and related activities of business take place, principally on the Internet.

> Study others' offers, reviewing the many ways other entrepreneurs collect their fees or part of them in advance, and see if you can apply the principle to your own practice. Don't be bound by the past but try to think creatively and boldly.

There are a great many other examples of imaginative entrepreneurs who have devised many ingenious ways to minimize costs, avoid costs, and get paid in advance. Here are a few examples that ought to suggest some ideas to you.

Joe Cossman is one of the legends of the mail order business. Enormously successful, as he deserves to be, here are a couple of principles he follows and advocates.

He set $500 as his top limit (he probably has raised that figure in these inflated times) to try out, test, and evaluate a new idea, and he usually spent less than that before deciding to go on with or drop the idea. He says that the one time he made an exception to that and set his limit higher, he lost $60,000.

He says, also, that you should get slightly sick to your stomach anytime you have to spend money, especially when you are spending money unnecessarily. You can get so much simply by asking for it, according to Cossman.

Let's take advertising, for instance. It's one of the most expensive (probably *the* most expensive) item in your budget. But you can get a great deal of free advertising. Free advertising is called *publicity*, and not only is it free but it is many times more effective than paid advertising. You can't buy the kind of advertising that publicity gives you.

 publicity informal name for public relations (PR); free advertising.

Cossman makes good use of publicity. He always manages to get reams of publicity for his products and promotions by being clever and resourceful, and by asking for it.

In other words, when you can get editors, publishers, TV talk show hosts, and others to give you free publicity, you are using their money for your advertising, money you do not have to pay back ever.

The trick is to give your product or promotion an angle. If it's truly new and different, use that angle. Write a story about it in a press release, for example, and tell what it does for users. Send that story out—with photos, if it's a product that needs illustrating—to editors, newspeople, and others who communicate with the public. But don't expect to get your story into *Time* magazine, unless it's truly unusual and you happen to get lucky. Settle for the trade press, those many magazines, newspapers, and newsletters that circulate among those in a given trade. (Go to the library and look them up. You will find them listed in reference books, such as *Writer's Market* and *Gale Directory of Publications and Broadcast Media.*) If you mail your story to enough of these, you will likely get publicity worth many times your cost in doing this.

In just one of my own promotions, for example, I sold books and newsletters dealing with selling to the federal government. I made many deals with associations and other newsletter and trade magazine publishers to get free publicity in their publications, while I gave their members and readers special discounts.

> Learn how to use publicity—write effective press releases and make up special offers for other entrepreneurs, for example—and take advantage of all the free advertising you can get this way.

OTHER CASH FLOW RESOURCES

There are some other simple and easy ways to handle some of your problems of financing and cash flow, if the sums you need are not great ones. They may cost you a bit more in interest charges than conventional business financing, but sometimes it is worth that cost to solve the immediate problem. Moreover, some of the expedients are much faster than applying for bank loans and represent, in fact, a small but standing and ever ready line of credit.

I refer to the premium Visa and MasterCard bank cards, which usually carry a $5,000 or higher limit each, and which enable you to do more than merely charge purchases to them: They also enable you to obtain cash at ATMs (automatic teller machines), and many provide checks that you can use as you would any check. You can have more than one of these cards, and use each independently of the others. Obviously, it is necessary to use these cards responsibly and avoid that hazard of becoming a credit-card junkie. The money is perhaps too easily available, and the interest rate is high; caution in use is essential.

If your business is such that you run open accounts with many of your clients and get into that problem of having too much money on the street, there is another alternative, one used by companies large and small. It is the practice of *discounting paper* or selling it, as some put it, to a lending institution. You may have noticed that when you bought a major appliance from your local dealer that you got a payment book later from some bank. The dealer discounted its note at the bank. That is, the bank bought your note by paying the dealer the money represented by the note you signed, less some percentage that became the lender's interest or profit on the transaction.

discounting paper
selling receivables as assets at a discounted rate to banks or other lenders.

You can do the same, although you will not have the bargaining power of Sears or the Ford Motor Company to get the most favorable terms. You may also have to agree to "recourse," meaning you are responsible for any accounts that prove to be uncollectible.

It is also possible that you will run into difficulties getting a commercial bank to handle your small account. As in the case of business loans, most banks are not especially fond of handling the accounts of small businesses, whose total volume is not very large. Although the U.S. Small Business Administration and, in many cases, local and state agencies help small businesses get loans, there is no equivalent program for discounting your receivables for cash. Therefore, you may wish to turn to individuals known as *factors*, who will buy your receivables, but only at a greater discount than that imposed by a bank.

factor
one who buys receivables at a higher discounted rate than banks or other lenders.

It is also helpful in several ways to be able to offer your own customers the convenience of using credit cards in making purchases from you, and it is not difficult to arrange this. You can become authorized to handle Visa and MasterCard charges at some local bank. When you deposit the slips they are like cash deposits: The money is immediately available, so that from the viewpoint of cash flow alone, charges are more convenient than checks. Also, of course, they are essentially without risk.

You will have to pay some fee for the privilege, depending on volume and prime rates in effect at the time, but there is a benefit in that the convenience to your customers helps encourage sales. Some people report as much as 25 percent of their sales are made on such charges.

OTHER APPROACHES

With care and the use of as many of these approaches as are applicable to your own venture, you should be able to solve most of your financing and cash flow problems. Later, we'll discuss other income sources, and that ought to suggest yet other ways to attack the cash flow problem and to obtain client participation in funding your practice.

Chapter

3

Insurance and Taxes

Death and taxes may be inevitable, but so are insurance and taxes in today's world. Taxes have been inevitable from the beginning of the first society of humans, and the need for insurance of several kinds is now almost as great as the need for air to breathe.

TAXES AND THE HOME OFFICE

One burden of all business is that you are required to pay taxes at many levels—federal, state, and local. Moreover, you get to (are required to) collect some of the taxes (sales tax, for example) for some of these many governments and you even get a pittance for doing so. On the other hand, a major advantage of doing business in and from your own residence is the tax benefit of being able to claim certain items as business deductions. If you understand the IRS rules and handle things properly, you can achieve a weighty chunk of relief in your tax burden by using part of your home for business purposes.

As in the case of discussing accounting systems earlier, I claim no expertise and certainly no special qualifying experience as a professional expert in the relevant field of taxes. For details and qualified legal opinions, you must consult a qualified public accountant and/or a lawyer. My experience is entirely as a taxpayer and business executive, and I do claim a fair amount of practice in those capacities; I have paid a variety of taxes to a variety of governments over a very long time! Despite my amateur standing as a commentator and mentor in tax matters, however, I can pass on some useful experience-based information to illustrate typical cases and my own personal fortunes and misfortunes in fencing with tax collectors.

Take your tax obligations seriously. Unpleasant adversarial encounters with the IRS will usually find you on the losing side. My personal experience is that if you respond to IRS inquiries honestly and objectively, the IRS will not usually be hostile or even overly aggressive. My encounters with the IRS have always reached a tolerable resolution, even on one occasion a more than reasonable concession by the IRS.

mythology
common beliefs that either are old wives' tales or are based on a tiny seed of fact, such as a single historical instance.

Also, again as in the case of accounting, there exists in the public mind at large a certain widespread *mythology*, naïveté, and plain wrongheadedness about taxes, tax obligations, and tax exemptions or deductions. Many myths have grown up, some with a tiny grain of truth at their base (but usually only a very tiny grain) extrapolated from some single occurrence somewhere at some time.

The consequences of believing some of these myths too readily and thus being wrong about these matters are sometimes quite unpleasant. Hence, I offer these observations about what I have learned and what you ought to do to verify any uncertainties you may have about what you may or may not do about your tax burdens. This is especially the case with regard to the main tax base, the one the IRS insists on collecting as a tax on our earnings.

Unfortunately, some of these phenomena of misunderstanding and plain ignorance of the tax laws are evident in the utterings and actions of the employees of tax offices as well as among the lay public. Even those who are charged with giving counsel and guidance to honest taxpayers can be mistaken in their interpretations of tax law and tax policy, and the IRS does not consider itself to be obligated by the false counsel of its own experts. For example, when I had a question as to the admissibility of expenses I incurred that exceeded the allowance made by my employer at that time, I was assured by an IRS counselor that I could deduct the excess. My plea of misleading guidance availed me absolutely nothing, as it fell on the stone-deaf ears of a tax official who disallowed my claim. I, of course, therefore urge caution in following the counsel of even the tax office employees. At the very least, double-check with someone else if you have any doubts about the advice you were given, even that coming from a tax official.

On the other hand, I have not found it to be true that all IRS agents are cruel, unscrupulous, and unforgiving, as so many taxpayers have reported in relating their own horror stories. In several brushes with the IRS, I have been able to establish an amiable relationship and reach a reasonable arrangement. The most important point in such discussions and negotiations: Do not allow your position or that of the tax officer to become polarized. Back off, if you appear to be getting to that point.

> Do not fight the IRS if you run afoul of it. Most of the time, if you are cooperative, the IRS will help you reach an acceptable outcome and solution to your tax problem.

Dedicated Space for Business

The most important tax question for anyone working in an independent venture at home is that of tax deductions for business expenses. The IRS policy is fairly clear on how much of your home expense you may deduct as a business expense. The basic principle is simple enough: The space you use for business and as a tax deduction must be dedicated, which means devoted exclusively to your business use. Opening the morning mail at your dining room table does not qualify you for a deduction of the dining room as a work space if you are still using it as a personal dining room. But you will find some exceptions to this seemingly clear-cut principle, although its application to special circumstances still makes good sense.

If you take some room of your residence and fit it out as a full-time business office or other business work space, you are on safe ground in claiming the cost of that space as a business deduction. You deduct the cost of that space on a prorated basis. For example, if you are maintaining a residence of 1,000 square feet and the room or rooms you convert for business use represent 250 square feet, you are entitled to deduct 25 percent of the cost (rent, taxes, interest, etc.) of that 1,000 square feet as a business expense.

When the space you dedicate for business use is not clearly separate, as in the case of using only part of a room, the distinction is less clear. But the principle still applies: The space must be used exclusively for business, as if it were at another location than one in your home, such as in an office building or industrial plant. But it becomes more difficult to demonstrate to an IRS auditor, should it become necessary, that the space that is only part of a room is truly dedicated to and used solely for business. If, for example, you use a portion of a room (such as a corner of your bedroom or basement) for business, you must somehow demonstrate clearly that the area is used exclusively for business. Do this by equipping the space with a desk, filing cabinet, workbench, or whatever furniture and equipment you need that is obviously suited to your business venture. Keep your personal items out of that area. If you can, separate it physically with a portable partition or room divider of some kind. The physical evidence of dedication will always be more convincing than your verbal arguments.

Principal Facility

With few exceptions, deduction of cost for work space in your home is allowable only when that space represents your principal place of business. If you have an office somewhere in an office building where you spend most of your time, you can deduct all of that cost as a business expense. However, you are not entitled also to deduct costs for desk space you use at home occasionally for business purposes, according to the IRS. (The IRS disallowed a surgeon deduction of the cost of an office in his home where he occasionally met with a patient because he did most of his meeting with patients and maintenance of his records at the hospital. He won in Tax Court, but the Supreme Court upheld the IRS.) Exceptions to this rule include professional people whose clients come to their homes, but this use requires face-to-face meetings with clients on a more or less regular basis to qualify. It is wise for a self-employed individual to avoid claiming two separate offices. The IRS will almost surely be skeptical. But there are also cases where individuals divide their time between an office at home and another elsewhere, and this is a normal and necessary business procedure. If you do this on a regular, scheduled basis, you can probably justify the home office expense. Or if you maintain an office somewhere and your spouse works with you as a partner but in an office in your home, you may have an arguable case for deducting the cost of that office at home. (Believe it or not, the IRS does not always win disputed cases such as these, and a firm stand on your part may very well pay off in a conciliatory IRS response.)

> Dedication of space and/or other facilities for business use is required to write off use of your personal domicile and facilities as business expenses, although you may rent to your business the use of personal property, such as an automobile.

Other Deductible Expenses

The basic cost of the space is usually the major tax deduction for an office at home, but it is not the only one.

You can deduct a reasonable portion of other expenses that are shared between your business and your personal life. If you keep a separate telephone line for business, its total cost is deductible; if your business shares your personal telephone line, prorate its cost. Apply this principle to all costs that are shared, such as those for water, trash collection, real estate taxes, interest on your mortgage, utilities, insurance on your property, maintenance of your property, and others. (Of course, insurance on business property only and maintenance of business property or business space only is fully deductible.)

This applies in principle to all items. If you buy new furniture and depreciate it over five years, that simply means that you take 20 percent of its cost as a business deduction each year. At the end of five years, you have recovered the cost of the furniture and take no more deductions for it, although it will probably be useful for years to come. But suppose you take to your office and use some old personal furniture that you have had for years and have charged your business for it by paying yourself some sum of money for it. It doesn't matter how old or even decrepit the furniture is; you can and should start a depreciation period on it as though it were new. Depreciation is an accounting convenience, a method for ensuring that the business is properly credited with an expense item represented by the furniture. It has nothing to do with real useful life of a capital item, but only with how you will charge its cost to the business—that is, primarily over how long a time you deduct and recover its cost as an investment.

That brings up the matter of expensing versus depreciating capital items. Expensing an item means writing it off in the year it was bought. Depreciating it means writing it off over several years, usually five or 10, more in the case of real estate. But it is applied to capital items, which are generally items costing above some specified amount and having a useful life of more than one year.

First of all, you must define what a capital item is in your own system. It is largely arbitrary. You set a value as the minimum, perhaps $200 or $500, and all items costing more than that amount and having an extended useful life are capitalized. If the item is within the IRS guidelines for maximum value of an item that may be expensed, you can write it off in the year you bought it. When I bought a modest computer system for $2,500, I chose to write it off immediately. The IRS permitted me to do so with any capital item not in excess of $5,000 cost, under the rules that year. (This is an accounting policy decision, but it is not out of place in this chapter because it illustrates that tax obligations have a great influence on accounting policies and procedures.)

> Within whatever overall limit the IRS sets, you can decide for yourself what a capital item is that you will expense—charge off completely in the year you buy it—and what you will depreciate—charge off over several years.

Limitations

If your business is a part-time venture and you have regular income from a job, you cannot use business tax deductions to offset taxes you owe on your income from that job. That is, the deductions you take for use of space and other facilities at home cannot exceed the gross income earned at home. If your home-based venture brought in $25,000 in gross profit and you had $26,000 worth of what would normally qualify as deductible expenses, you may still deduct only $25,000. Thus you have no business profit to tax, and you have a loss, at least on paper.

That brings up another interesting point: When is an at-home venture, especially a part-time one, a business and when is it merely a hobby? The IRS position on this has been that your home-based business may show losses or, at least, zero profit for three years at most. After that, if it continues to show no profit, the IRS believes

**conventional
wisdom**
that which is
believed to be
generally true
and valuable as a
guideline.

that your activity is a hobby and not a business venture at all. On the other hand, venture capitalists who invest and risk large sums of money on others' ventures tend toward the *conventional wisdom* that it is not unreasonable for a new venture to require three or four years to reach breakeven and begin to show a small profit. But, of course, the position of a venture capitalist is a bit different than that of an individual trying to establish a business at home. In any case, be prepared for the IRS to be somewhat jaundiced in its view of your deductions for a venture that is not earning or about to earn profits by the end of a third year.

State and Local Taxes

By now, a great many state and local governments impose a sales tax on their citizens, and they normally demand that the retailer collect the tax for them, allowing the retailer-cum-tax-collector 1 or 2 percent of what he or she collects. Of course, the retailer would far prefer not to be bothered with the sales tax at all, but the government would almost surely collect virtually nothing if each citizen was expected to calculate and pay 2, 3, or 5 percent of everything he or she spends to acquire title to worldly goods. So it is necessary to burden the seller with the problem and unpleasant duty. That means that you do not pay the sales tax when you buy your materials or products if you buy them for resale, but you require your own customers to do so.

Generally, when you register with your government and get a tax number—a certificate and identification as a seller who will collect taxes and turn them over to the government—you are exempt from paying the tax yourself, under the assumption that you buy the goods for resale and your customers will pay the sales tax. When you buy your products or supplies you furnish your tax number as an exemption, and your supplier does not charge you. For example, if you buy cosmetics in bulk and repackage them to sell to consumers, you are exempted from paying the sales tax on what you buy because you are going to charge your own customers tax and turn that money over to your government.

The principle applies also to raw material or unfinished goods: Whether you buy and resell finished goods or buy materials that somehow go into the finished goods you sell, you are exempt from paying the sales tax until you have collected it from your own customers—or you may never pay the sales tax if you are not the seller to the consumer but rather sell to those who sell to consumers, because in that case your customers must collect the taxes from the ultimate consumers.

> If your state has a sales tax and the sales tax covers any product or service you sell, you will probably need to get a tax number and collect the sales tax for your state government.

A Few Miscellaneous Taxes

Of course, the income tax is the big tax bite, but for the self-employed today, the Social Security tax is no small consideration, either. In fact, for many individuals the FICA (Federal Insurance Contributions Act) tax is even greater than the income tax because there are no exemptions or deductions on FICA. It is levied on gross income to the maximum provided by law.

When you are employed by someone, you pay one half, well over 7 percent of your earnings up to the maximum, and your employer pays the other half. When you are incorporated, you pay both halves: You are an employee of your own corporation and handled on paper as such, getting a W-2 form, for example, as when you work for anyone. Your corporation pays the matching FICA. If you are in a self-employed status (unincorporated), you still pay the total amount (currently 15.02 percent) as a "self-employment tax."

There are some miscellaneous taxes, such as that for

unemployment benefits, but they are more an annoyance of extra recordkeeping and reporting than a financial burden.

The complex of taxes grows steadily more complex, so that it is more than the question of difficulty that impels most home-based businesspeople to seek professional help with taxes; the sheer amount of work required is itself a burden when you are struggling to get your main work done every day.

Special Situations

There has been a trend to the steady elimination or relaxing of laws that have prevented employers from having employees work at home on piecework and other arrangements. In fact, except for the garment industry (the classic historical case of child labor laws), most of the relevant laws are gone or greatly moderated. Thus an increasing number of situations may enable you to deduct home office and other expenses even when you are not self-employed. (Many independent consultants accept work as temporaries, and may even work at home in that capacity.) For example, if your services include telephone solicitation on a commission basis from your own office at home, and that place of work is a required condition of the job, you can probably qualify for a tax deduction. The office must meet the conditions described earlier, and you must not have been compensated by the employer for any expenses of maintaining an office, telephone, and other costs necessary to your work.

> Whatever is absolutely necessary to the work you do at home and is not directly compensated by an employer or client—tools, special clothing, training, manuals, utilities, shipping, postage, equipment, repairs, or other items—is probably deductible.

INSURANCE

Again, I am compelled to furnish the now familiar preamble that I speak about insurance from personal experience only, and not as an expert on insurance. In fact, I have often been mystified by the language of the policies and the explanations of the agents. Like most people, I have tended to throw up my hands in the face of this incomprehensible phraseology and to accept what I was being told. That may or may not have been a sensible thing to do, but it has appeared to be the only practicable course open to me at the time. And so I must stand before you as not even a dilettante in the field, much less an expert, and relate my notions gained from my own experience.

In this case, that may be an advantage to you because I have no axes to grind here: I am neither a champion of, an apologist for, nor a critic of the insurance industry. Quite the contrary, I'll try to be entirely objective in discussing insurance generally, within the limits of my understanding of this quite arcane field. Fortunately, I have had both good and bad experiences with insurance companies, and that helps me to present a reasonably balanced view.

We must accept that insurance has become inescapable in today's world. Two factors make it absolutely necessary to maintain insurance policies of several kinds: First, ours has become an excessively litigious society, and second, the costs of almost everything have skyrocketed. Nor are these two considerations unrelated to each other, for the cost of defending yourself in a legal battle, even when you are entirely blameless and end up winning the suit, can easily mean financial ruin. ("Winning" can be a sardonic term, with definite Pyrrhic overtones.) It has, in fact, meant just that for many individuals. But everything is excessively costly today, and a loss through burglary, fire, or other casualty loss can impose an intolerable burden on you and on your business venture.

The kinds of insurance you need depend to at least some extent on the nature of your venture. Some businesses, for example, include significant possibilities of being sued for large sums of money. That means you must have liability insurance, and in large enough amounts to protect you adequately against a judgment. Suppose you package and sell some kind of consumer product, perhaps some kind of computer software. What are the possibilities that a customer might sue you for damages? They are probably not great, for computer software is not likely to injure anyone seriously. But there is the possibility that some other packager of software may decide that you have infringed on his or her copyright or trade name, and decide to sue you. (Such occurrences are not at all rare today.)

So serious is the problem of liability and related litigation today that rates for coverage in some fields have reached critical levels. Many lawyers and physicians, the latter especially, have found that they simply cannot afford the malpractice insurance necessary today and have quit their private practices. So it is a matter for careful consideration: Many people, perhaps almost all, need some kind of liability insurance.

Probably you maintain some kind of general coverage for liability in the event someone is injured on your property, as well as general fire and burglary coverage. These may or may not protect you. You must check them carefully to see what restrictions they include. They may, for example, exclude coverage if your property is used for business purposes or they may include limits that are not adequate. In my own case, for example, extra policies cover the computer, fax, and other special equipment used to conduct my freelance writing activities. I also insist on having policies that will pay full replacement value, rather than some depreciated value that would reimburse only a fraction of what was paid out for the property and what it would cost to replace it. For example, we were burglarized some years ago, and we recovered only about one-third of the original value of what had been stolen, so we were put to considerable expense to replace our property, despite insurance.

> Be careful about what your insurance does and does not provide you in the way of protection against losses. Do not hesitate to ask your insurance broker as many direct questions as you need to get answers you fully understand.

Group Insurance

Health insurance is as much of a must today as are all other categories of coverage, for a health or sickness problem can do you in financially as quickly as can a lawsuit or major casualty loss, if uncovered and uncompensated. My own unexpected, lengthy illness some years ago resulted in medical expenses of over $40,000 in a few weeks. We would have been in straits for some time paying that bill had we not been covered adequately.

The answer to this need for coverage for hospital and major medical emergencies is group insurance of some kind. It is a necessity for most of us, who could otherwise never afford the cost of a hospital stay of even short duration. The problem is that a one- or two-person business is hardly a group, for insurance purposes. But there are numerous approaches to finding a solution.

The usual solution, a quite practical one, is to join a group via another group connection. One such connection usually available to you is membership in a trade or professional association of some sort. Many of these have today set up plans to provide group insurance to members. But it does not have to be an association connected with your business. It can be via an automobile club, a veterans group, or even an ad hoc group organized entirely for group insurance coverage. Today, most sponsors of such coverage will accept groups of as few as six members, although it is always a good idea to form or join as large a group as possible.

There is always the possibility that you may continue coverage under an older policy that covered you in prior employment or under the policy of a spouse already employed and covered elsewhere. In my own case, my wife had been a government employee and belonged to a large HMO (health maintenance organization). We have belonged to this together, under direct billing, ever since.

> Getting health insurance is a major problem for many self-employed individuals. If you already belong a group through former employment, try to convert that to use, if possible. Otherwise, investigate the benefits of joining an association to gain admission to a group for health insurance purposes.

Disability Insurance

The self-employed individual has no sick leave; you must get sick on your own time. That means without compensation, of course: When you are ill, your earnings stop. For brief illnesses of a few days, that is tolerable; for lengthy illnesses, it is not.

There is insurance to guard against the worst effects of this: disability insurance, which is insurance that will provide you with an income in some prescribed amount for some prescribed period of time when illness or accident renders you incapable of working. If you are entirely dependent on your earnings from your business venture, it would probably be most wise to investigate disability insurance and sign up for a policy.

Policies vary widely in how much they cost and the benefits they provide, and these two factors are related to each other, of course. You must find some acceptable balance between the minimum set of benefits acceptable to you and the maximum cost you can afford.

Miscellaneous Insurance

The foregoing is by no means a complete description or discussion of all kinds of insurance of interest, although it does cover the major categories. If you are in a partnership, you may wish to insure both partners so that the succeeding partner is protected against heirs taking over a deceased partner's interest and harming the enterprise or otherwise making continuance of participation difficult for you as the surviving partner. This insurance may provide the means for paying off heirs and assuming complete ownership, for example, or for getting out yourself. There is also product liability insurance and special insurance coverage of other kinds.

Choosing Insurance and Insurers

The insurance industry is regulated in every state by an insurance commission of some sort. These agencies are supposed to protect the common welfare with regard to insurance because hardly any layperson is capable of fully understanding either the language or the laws concerning insurance. And yet you cannot rely on these commissions to protect you against predatory underwriters: Some are quite honorable, quick to honor their contracts, while there are some who are not, who try to find ways to evade their contractual obligations. I personally had excellent experiences with two who paid claims cheerfully and quickly and even urged me to send in every scrap of paper because I might have additional coverage I was not aware of. (I did, and was sent an additional check.) But I had quite distressing experiences with others, who struggled to avoid paying claims and sometimes succeeded in doing so.

Predators in the insurance industry appear to be especially active in the areas of health and disability insurance. You would be wise to move cautiously in buying this kind of insurance. And one way is to buy insurance through established brokers either whom you know or that have been highly recommended by friends who do know them well. Brokers have a vested interest in protecting your interest, for you are *their* customers. Our own insurance broker has been writing all our insurance for more than a few years, and he will continue to do so because he is more than an insurance broker or agent: He is our friend and protector in matters of insurance. He guides us away from mistakes in insurance and works hard to explain to us why he recommends what he does. He listens carefully to what we want, and then counsels us accordingly. If we have a claim, he handles it, fighting our insurance battles for us, if necessary. We feel comfortable with Jerry. He handles all our insurance problems quietly and efficiently, so that we can concentrate on doing what we do for a living.

My own experience has been that it is best to use an independent insurance broker. One handles all my insurance, and I have relied on his advice for years with complete satisfaction.

Chapter

4

Pricing Your Services

Pricing your independent consulting services is not an easy matter to resolve, as you shall soon learn when you examine all sides of the many questions involved.

TWO BASIC APPROACHES

As you have read earlier in these pages, defining independent consulting is not easy, but it is clear that there are two basic ways independent consultants provide services to clients. Or, to put it in another highly significant way, there are two basic roles the independent consultant plays in providing services. One role is that of an independent contractor. The other role is that of a temporary employee. But even that can be confusing, for you may contract directly with a client to work as a temporary employee or you may sign as a temporary employee of a *broker* who then assigns you to work on the premises of a client under the client's direction. Or, in yet another variation, you may sign a subcontract with a prime contractor, your contract requiring you to work on the premises of the prime contractor's client. On the other hand, you may sign a contract or subcontract to undertake a project for your client or the prime contractor's client and thus be re-

 broker
one who arranges transactions for a commission or other compensation; also one supplying temporaries, in which case may also be referred to sardonically as a "job shop," "body shop," or supplier of "warm bodies."

sponsible for the entire project. However, despite these complicating factors, either you will be a client's temporary employee or you will be under contract to carry out a complete project for the client. In the latter case, the client has described some service or objective to be achieved, and you have contracted as an independent contractor to deliver the client's desired result, using whatever means and working at whatever location(s) you choose, and charging whatever fees or rates you and the client have agreed on. These variables are most significant, as you shall see, but the major point to be made here is that when you contract to carry out a project, you make your own decisions on working hours, work sites, schedules, and all other matters not prescribed specifically in your contract.

> Despite a number of complicating variables in arrangements you can make with clients to provide your services, there are only two basic roles you can play in serving clients: You are either a temporary employee or you are an independent contractor. Never lose sight of this distinction and the pros and cons of each.

There is an important distinction to be pointed out with regard to the role you assume in providing your services as an hourly employee (albeit temporary) or as an independent contractor of a project. The difference is quite significant in more than one way, but probably in none more important than how it affects your pricing and fees. It is necessary to explore the several working situations beyond the most basic introduction given earlier in these pages, if you want to fully understand and appreciate the choices you have and how they affect the benefits you can gain from your consulting practice.

Temporary Employee versus Independent Contractor = W-2 versus 1099

An employee must always be issued a Form W-2 by the employer at the end of a calendar year, and another copy of that form is sent to the IRS. The form lists the employee's earnings and taxes withheld, which leads to referring informally to the individual's status as that of a W-2. A contractor is issued a Form 1099 by a client at the end of the year, listing the money paid to the contractor by the client, and a copy of that form goes to the IRS. This leads to a casual identification of the contractor's status as a *1099*.

Many independent consultants consider themselves to be independent contractors, which would presumably confer on them the right to file tax returns as independent businesses, qualified to deduct all business expenses. For a number of years, however, the IRS has not fully agreed with this. Where a consultant has performed all work on the client's premises, used the client's facilities, worked the client's business hours, taken direct supervision from the client, and/or given any of 20 such indications of being an employee, the IRS has disallowed business deductions and insisted on the individual filing as an employed person, regardless of pricing and billing arrangements. This has led to an increase in consultants taking the path of least resistance, the easy way out, by opting to enter temporary employment by organizations that provide temporary help to clients. (This is one of the factors, along with economic considerations, that has led to a steady growth in the temporary labor industry.) From the consultant's perspective, this may be a shortsighted expedient, offering a quick and easy solution that may not be the best one.

1099 form issued to independent contractor by client listing total sum paid to independent contractor during the year; also term used to identify consultant informally as independent contractor, filing tax forms as independent business.

THE CHOICES

There are cases in which you, as the consultant, will have little choice but to accept the assignment as offered or decline the assignment, but in more general terms you always have a choice. That is, you may decide in advance that you will or will not accept temporary employment as your role in delivering consultant services, and will or will not insist on accepting only independent contracts to carry out projects for clients. Some independent consultants establish firm rules with regard to how they will work. You may do so also, or, like many independent consultants, you may prefer independent contracting but accept assignments as a temporary employee when that is all that is available at the moment.

> There are most definitely pros and cons to each choice—temporary employee or independent contractor. You can make the choice in advance by setting a policy on what role you will accept as an independent consultant, or you can make the choice on a case-by-case basis.

HOW PRICING IS AFFECTED

As a W-2, you are normally paid as an hourly employee at some rate consistent with what others are paid for similar work and responsibilities. You are thus pretty much at the mercy of whatever is the going rate in your area and industry for the kind of work you do. In fact, you are usually offered the assignment at some stipulated rate. Whether that rate is negotiable depends on certain key factors. One factor is your personal reputation. If that is impressive enough, it does furnish some leverage. Other factors are your credentials and how impressive they are, the general availability of labor for that assignment, and the urgency of the assignment. And still another factor is your negotiating skill. Even so and given the best of circumstances, there is a limit to how much the rate can be adjusted via negotiation. The top rate will still be confined to the general ballpark as a limiting factor.

On the other hand, as an independent contractor undertaking a project, you price the job yourself. That may be at some hourly or daily *billing rate*, which would include your overhead, all costs, and profit markup, or you may choose to quote a firm, fixed price for the entire job. Of course, the client may prefer one or the other method and may even insist on whatever is the client's choice of billing.

billing rates
standard rates charged clients per hour or per day for consulting services; other rates may exist for ancillary services.

Therein (in the choice of costing and billing a project) lies a matter open to dispute among independent consultants with whom I have discussed this subject. A great many independent consultants, probably a large majority in fact, balk sharply at the very idea of quoting a firm, fixed price because they see such a quotation as placing them at great risk. They foresee the possibility—even the probability, apparently—of their having underestimated the job, the client making demands well beyond the original scope of the project, or their being forced to do far more work than they anticipated and planned when they estimated the project and the time and material to complete it. On the other hand, they see a riskless project when they quote an hourly or daily billing rate, meaning a project that goes on, open-ended, producing income for the consultant indefinitely until the client is satisfied.

When you quote a firm, fixed price for the job, you are assuming total responsibility for the successful completion of the project, responsibility to produce the result the client has asked for, at the price you quoted. But when you are retained at an hourly billing rate, you are responsible only for being on the job as required and delivering the work for the hours or days you bill the client. Taking on project responsibility means assuming risk; working on an hourly rate means no risk.

> The question of whether you will quote a firm, fixed price for the job or work only for an hourly rate (as a matter of your policy or in making the decision on a case-by-case basis) turns on whether you are willing to accept responsibility for a project or only responsibility for being on the job and providing your services on an hourly or daily basis.

THE NEED FOR SPECIFICATIONS

specifications
precise and complete details of what is to be done and results required in both qualitative and quantitative terms.

The fear is well founded because so few independent consultants prepare a proposal or even a simple but complete set of *specifications* of the project for which they quote a price. It is that set of specifications, primarily quantifying what is to be delivered for the dollars quoted (what, exactly, the client is entitled to for a certain price) that is needed to nullify or at least minimize the risks normally incurred when accepting a project. The lack of specifications leaves entirely open the identification of the completion of the project. The client is thus entirely justified in deciding when the project is complete and when more effort is required. In short, that lack of specification invites—even begs for—disputes, and it is clear enough that the client has all the strength in a dispute. On the other hand, when the contract states clearly that the client will receive a sales manual of 200 pages, plus or minus 10 percent, with one opportunity to review the draft and request changes, the client's freedom to ask for more is clearly limited, except by renegotiation of the contract, stipulated in a *changes* clause in the contract. That is what puts you in an equal position with the client in the event of dispute.

change
a change in requirement or other element that requires an amendment to the contract.

This subject of specifications and responsibilities is not confined to rates and pricing, but has relevance to many other matters of interest; therefore, discussions to be found elsewhere in these pages will shed additional light on the subject of projects and specifications. One important point, however, is this: In some cases, preparing detailed

> The chief reason for fear of being responsible for an entire project—financial risk—is valid enough, but it can be easily overcome by always accompanying a firm, fixed price quotation with a clear set of specifications. That tells the client clearly what he or she is entitled to expect for the dollars quoted.

specifications can be a laborious and time-consuming job, which means it is an expensive job more often than not. For that reason, many consultants avoid it, and therefore avoid undertaking projects. Clients are also often reluctant (or simply unequipped) to provide any but relatively general and vague specifications of what they wish to have done or developed. So, too often contracts are let without proper specification. One way some consultants handle this problem successfully is to explain the need for and advantages to the client of having a set of detailed specifications, and offer to develop a set of specifications as the first task of the contract or, if necessary, as a separate preliminary contract.

> Sometimes you can persuade a client to pay you to develop a set of specifications as the first task of the contract or as a separate contract.

PROS OF WORKING FOR HOURLY RATES

Many independent consultants look at independent consulting as the opportunity to work at much higher hourly rates than they could realize as permanent employees, in exchange for giving up the fringe benefits that regular employment normally includes. (That is the norm.) They soon learn that "temporary" is a relative term: There are many cases where temporary assignment goes on for years, so longevity of employment is not always a concern. Of course, many independent consultants have recently left regular employment and so have a salaried or hourly orientation that makes them judge and evaluate employment only against the yardstick of those measures.

PROS OF A FIRM, FIXED PRICE

The major negative factor in offering a firm, fixed price has been described, but the major positive factor has not yet been identified. It is this: It frees you from the limitations of an hourly rate (i.e., the clients' expectation that you will work for whatever is the going hourly rate in your area, even if that is unrealistically low). Normally, when a client agrees to contract for a fixed price, the client wants to know with some detail what you will do, rather than how well qualified you are. That leads to a technical evaluation of what you offer, rather than a pure price comparison, and so gives you the opportunity to sell your offer in a proposal, that major selling tool of custom services. That creation of a special opportunity to sell your services on the basis of quality, rather than price, is one major advantage; the other is the opportunity for greater profit in pricing your services, greater independence, and thus greater growth of your business.

Undertaking total project responsibility by contracting to complete the project for a fixed price makes you a truly independent contractor as a consultant, rather than an hourly employee. It puts you in command of the project, and gives you much greater opportunity for growth of your business.

ALTERNATIVES OPEN TO YOU

The practical truth is, as suggested earlier in this chapter, that you do not always have the freedom of choice. Clients have their own ideas about what they want, and many have already been influenced by the common practice of hiring consultants as temporary hourly employees or under fixed-price contracts. (Clients, like most of us, tend almost automatically to favor the familiar and resist change to the unfamiliar.) You may thus routinely reject some bidding opportunities as contradictory to your firm policy, or you may make decisions on a case-by-case basis, as pointed out earlier. However, you also have other possibilities: You may always try to sell the client on contracting via whatever mode is your preference, making a direct sales argument for your preferred contracting basis. Or, as an alternative to that, you may offer the client a choice by presenting plans for contracting both ways, leaving the choice to the client after making your case in that presentation. A written proposal is the proper vehicle for carrying out one of these latter two suggestions, and you should consider this seriously.

> If you agree that fixed-price contracting for projects is the better way, you can always try to sell the idea to prospective clients. (You are, after all, a sales professional.) Use a written proposal for this.

BILLABLE HOURS

When you work for an organization on a regular basis as a permanent employee, you can expect to work 40 hours per week every week and thus get paid for 2,080 hours every year (ignoring overtime, if that is a factor in your job). When you work as a temporary, you may or may not work 2,080 hours annually. While many temporary jobs continue for several years, most do not. Most are for a period of weeks or months. Even so, some consultants who accept such assignments manage to work every week of the year, even if for more than one employer, but you probably cannot count on doing this. You probably should plan to be employed an average of about 20 percent fewer hours than this, with about 1,600 billable hours per year. The difference will be the time you spend between assignments, interviewing, and sending out resumes. You may be using some of that time for your own vacations and other time off.

An analogous situation exists when you contract for fixed-price projects as an independent contractor. You may allocate yourself 50 hours a week or 2,600 hours per year as the hours available to you for work, but not all those hours are income-producing because not all are billable hours, hours for which you charge clients. You will spend some hours doing overhead work, probably spending at least one-third of those hours in marketing and administration, and many consultants find that they have not much more than 1,000 hours they can bill to clients each year. Be conscious of that probability when you estimate your projects and the amount of your time you will spend doing the work of that project. For example, if your plan includes paying yourself $75,000 per year, you would have to count on billing clients $150 for every hour to allow for the burden of overhead and other direct costs. (Your actual figures may be significantly different from the guesstimates offered here.)

You may find it a good idea to keep close track of what you are doing in both billable and nonbillable hours. See what nonbillable hours have cost you in income that you might have otherwise produced in those hours. Study billable hours to determine what work it was not really necessary for you to have done yourself, but could have paid someone else—perhaps an accountant, a secretary, or a technical writer—to do for you, and see whether you might not have been practicing a false economy in doing it yourself.

THE BASIS FOR ALL PRICING

Regardless of whether you are quoting an hourly or daily direct rate, an hourly or daily billing rate, or a fixed price, you must set the price by the reality of costs and necessary markup, not simply by estimating going rates or other guesstimates or trying to determine what the traffic will bear. In general, that basis includes *all* your costs and some acceptable profit markup. That immediately brings up the question of what are costs, not always as simple a question to answer as you may think.

Labor Costs

One place that individuals who are new to self-employment often err immediately is in determining where on the ledger should be posted their personal income drawn from their business. Those who are in the employ of a labor broker have no problem with this, for they are employees (W-2 workers), not independent contractors who are entitled to take business deductions, so they have no business costs and need not keep books. Whatever they are paid is net income to them. On the other hand, when such individuals do function as independent contractors, they tend to regard as profit whatever dollars they take home from the business as personal income or personal salary. That is a great mistake, as even rudimentary knowledge of accounting would quickly show. If you are incorporated, you are legally an employee of your corporation and must be treated as such. But even if you are a sole proprietor, you should regard your business as an entity of its own, of which you are an employee drawing a salary. That salary is not profit; it is cost—labor cost— just as it would be if you were paying it to a stranger you employed. Profit is not realized until you have recovered all costs, including your own compensation.

> Understand and never lose sight of the fact that your practice—your business—and you personally are two separate entities. Thus you work as an employee of your business, and any salary or personal draw you take from your practice is cost, not profit.

A question that arises naturally at this point is, "What if the business does not allow me to pay myself a regular salary?" That is, of course, an almost automatic question when the practice is new and not yet producing very much income. There are at least three possible answers to this question:

1. Pay your own salary out of your operating capital, if you have enough such capital, and charge the expense to overhead; or treat it as a personal loan to the business, to be repaid to you when the business can do so.
2. Forgo your salary, but put it down on the books as owed to you—a debit item—to be paid to you when possible, as in item 1.
3. Adjust your salary to whatever your business can pay you.

Even if the business can never pay you, items 1 and 2 keep your books straight so you'll be able to get a realistic idea of costs. (This assumes that you have a reasonable amount of billable time so that you are not running an unrealistically excessive overhead.) Item 3, of course, does not do so and is the least desirable solution.

Normally, your own salary will be the major cost item in your budget, since it is primarily your own labor that you sell. That does not mean that your salary is the only labor cost. Many independent consultants employ their own spouses, at least on a part-time basis, and everything that was said about your personal draw or salary is equally true for salary paid to a part-time worker, even a spouse who does not demand actual payment. Nor does it mean that there are not other costs, or that other costs are not significant items. Large accounting systems classify costs in a number of different kinds of groupings, but for our purposes here, the classifications will be kept simple, as in fact they usually are for a small business.

Cost Items That Make Up a Billing Rate

The costs we referred to earlier are *direct labor* costs. That is, they are costs of labor that you sell to the client. You may pay yourself or an employee $30 per hour, but your accounting system reveals that you must add $15 of your overhead to that figure to recover all your costs, so that you must charge clients $45 per hour for your labor. That does not include profit, so if your system includes a 15 percent pretax profit, you must add another $6.75 to that figure and bill your client $51.75 per hour.

That is the general case, but there are often other cost factors. If your spouse works part-time in helping you, you must determine whether your spouse's labor should be charged to the client as direct labor or as overhead. That comes down to determining whether your spouse worked directly on an assignment or worked only on general matters (*indirect labor*), such as answering the telephone, posting ledgers, and sending out invoices. In most cases, the spouse's work will include both direct and indirect time. In that case, you must keep a separate record of your spouse's direct time and charge the account accordingly, if you want an accurate record of how your business is really doing.

To be very clear, let us define direct, indirect, and overhead; it is important that you have a clear understanding of these. As you may have deduced by now, any cost that results directly from the requirements of a client's project and is attributable solely to that project is a direct cost. Labor is a major class of direct costs, but there can be others, such as travel, printing, and toll call charges incurred as part of the completion of a project. Any cost

direct labor
labor applied directly to client's work, costs of which are billable to client.

indirect labor
labor not billable directly to clients, the costs of which are recovered in the overhead charge.

that you cannot attribute directly to a project is an indirect cost. Normally, in a small business, all indirect costs are part of the overhead and taken together make up the overhead, so for our purposes the two terms mean the same thing. But that does not define overhead properly.

Overhead Rates, Historical and Provisional

Overhead is cost that you cannot attribute or assign to any single client or project, but is a general cost necessary to conduct your business, or to be ready to conduct business even when you are idle. Rent is one such cost. It goes on, regardless of how busy you are or are not. Your business must recover that cost, but how do you decide how much of the rent should be charged to Client A's project and how much should be charged to Client B's project? The same question applies to heat, light, postage, insurance, taxes, marketing, idle time, time devoted to management and administrative tasks, and other indirect items, all of which are part of your overhead pool—that entire collection of indirect cost items.

Here is how the problem of recovering those costs in your billing is resolved in the kind of accounting system you would normally use (i.e., historical rate): All indirect/ overhead costs for the year are added up and compared with the sum of direct labor costs to determine the rate of overhead as compared with direct labor. If, for example, you had a total cost of $32,000 in overhead and $60,000 in direct labor for the year, your overhead rate would be $32,000 divided by $60,000, or 53.3333 percent. In practice, you would probably round this up to 54 percent, adding 54 cents to every dollar of direct labor when you bill the client, plus your other direct costs, if any, and your profit factor; so you will recover all your indirect/ overhead costs on a prorated basis, each client being billed a share in proportion to the amount of direct labor the client's project required. (With direct labor the major direct cost, this results in a fair allocation of overhead cost. However, businesses that have a lot of direct material costs may have material overhead, and businesses that have both material and labor direct costs in significant quantity will usually have both material and labor overhead.)

What if you are in your first year of doing business and do not yet know what your year's overhead costs will be? In that case, you use a provisional—estimated—rate of overhead, rather than the historical rate just described. In fact, you will thereafter always be using the prior year's historical overhead figures, for they are the only ones you have.

Overhead as a Factor of Success

You will read and hear frequently of overhead as a business hazard. That refers to allowing overhead to grow and become an excessively burdensome expense. Over time, and especially in times when business is good, there is tendency to become careless and even generous in charging things to overhead—a costly Christmas party, liberal expense allowances, excessive idle time, keeping help you don't have enough work for, and dozens of other such items. Overhead thus creeps up until one day you suddenly find that your costs have accelerated and your profits declined or even turned into losses because of runaway overhead expenses. That is when you begin frantically to pare away the excess that should not have been permitted to grow. For any business organization, but for the small business especially, keeping overhead to a minimum is essential for success. Be ever conscious of overhead, and in reviewing your accounts always remember to scan overhead figures with an eye to changes, especially increases, as red flags.

A FEW TIPS ON ESTIMATING COSTS

There is no escaping the need to estimate in calculating costs and setting prices. The overhead rate you use, for example, is usually based on last year's figures and your assumption that the rate will not have changed materially since. But if you have some reason to believe that your true overhead rate is currently quite different from your historical rate, you will have to estimate the amount of change and the true current rate. In some cases, you need to have specifications to support your estimating, and the assumption here is that either you have specifications of some sort or the project is technically simple enough for you to infer specifications and use them as a basis for your estimates.

The risk in bidding a fixed price for a project actually is the risk that is inherent in estimating, which is inevitably based on making certain assumptions. When you estimate how many hours or days a certain task will take to complete, you base your estimate on what similar tasks have required in the past, especially when you do not have more reliable information. You may even add something as a margin for error, but, again, that is an estimate.

The greatest danger in estimating is using something too general, such as a gut feeling or an overall estimate of what similar projects have required in the past. For that reason, I use a series of successive approximations, rather than an overall ballpark estimate. I plan the project in as much detail as possible—breaking the whole project into a series of tasks—and estimate each task individually. I believe I have a much better likelihood of making an accurate estimate looking at small tasks. However, that aside, each estimate I make has, presumably, an equal chance of being an overestimate or being an underestimate. With a large number of estimates, I feel there is a mathematical probability that over and under errors will cancel each other out. That is the rationale for preferring a series of approximations to single, large estimates.

I thus break down the project into phases and tasks and estimate the probable effort required for each task in each phase. This is serious work, but it is risky to estimate any project cost without having a clear idea of exactly what is involved in carrying out the project. My estimate overall is thus based on rational analysis of each task individually. (I would not trust an estimate that was not based on a detailed plan for carrying out the project and estimates of each task in the plan.)

> Your own labor is your major cost item. To get the most accurate idea of how much labor is necessary for a project, plan the project in advance as a series of tasks and estimate each one individually, adding them together. This gives you the most accurate total estimate.

Only then do I consider other ways to arrive at an estimate for the entire project, such as the gut feeling and what similar projects with which I am familiar cost to complete. I compare those with the estimate I had arrived at. That comparison is an aid in validating the estimate I prepared so carefully by planning the project. And if I can think of yet another way of estimating the project, I will do that and again use the result as a means of validating my original estimate.

There is another important aid to planning a project. That aid is, in fact, at the heart of my project-planning methods and is a must for me when I undertake to write a proposal and present a detailed plan to a client. It is planning the project via a detailed functional *flowchart*, a process that will be explained later (Chapter 8) in connection with guidance in proposal writing.

DISCOUNTING FOR PROMPT PAYMENT

It is a common practice in the business world to allow clients a small discount, typically from 0.5 percent to 2 percent, for payment of invoices within 10 days. That is, of course, an effort to improve one's cash flow by speeding up payment. Unfortunately, many independent consultants report that clients too often accept the discount and

flowchart chart showing sequential steps and interrelationships of various procedures or phases in the conduct of a project; useful for estimating, planning, and explaining projects to clients.

still take 30 or more days to pay. For that reason, they have abandoned the offer of prompt payment discounts. And because of that common experience (which I share) I cannot recommend it, either.

SETTING YOUR RATES

We have discussed rates here, basically the several alternative bases for charging clients and the costs that must be recovered by the rates. All the discussions, so far, have been based on conventional cost accounting and conservative thinking, which means being competitive with your rates—in line, that is, with the rates charged by most other independent sales consultants. There is, however, another, entirely different school of thought on how to set your rates for best results as an independent entrepreneur, and this kind of thought leads to an entirely different basis for setting your rates and an entirely different set of rates. You will certainly encounter cases of other independent consultants basing their rates on this alternative method sooner or later. It could be a great shock to discover that you have competitors who do the same kind of work you do, offer clients no more and no less than you do, but get several times the rates you get and yet stay busy doing so. In fact, they are usually busier than you are, often turning work away. And that is one reason that these competitors charge those elevated rates.

> You will soon discover that a few of your competitors (a very few, in fact) charge and get much higher rates than most sales consultants do. What's more, they are kept quite busy with demands for their services.

One independent consultant explained to me how he came to set his rates so much higher than the rates other consultants were charging: He had become so busy that he could not handle all the work, and did not choose to hire help or associate himself with other consultants. He chose, instead, the simple solution of turning down the excess work. But how to decide what was excess? He solved this problem easily by raising his rates until the workload was manageable. Some clients left to seek less expensive services, so their work automatically became the "excess" work that he could not handle!

Not everyone is driven by circumstance to raise their rates. Other consultants begin to raise their rates (or start their practices at much higher rates than others charge) because they decide that neither they nor most of their direct competitors are charging clients enough for what they do. Almost without exception, those consultants who have so set their rates in the stratosphere find a great many differences in their daily working experience. Here are some of the comments made by consultants who raised their rates, not minimally but by large leaps from what they once thought was competitive:

- ✔ Instead of reducing demand for my services, higher rates *increased* the demand.
- ✔ I find myself closing sales much more easily at the higher rates.
- ✔ Marketing in general is easier than ever.
- ✔ My clients are much less demanding.
- ✔ I am treated with much greater respect.
- ✔ I get few complaints or callbacks.
- ✔ Recommendations and referrals are much greater.
- ✔ My visibility is greater than ever since my rates raised some eyebrows.

> Significantly higher rates bring about surprising and most pleasantly beneficial changes in independent consultants' workaday experiences.

That first example of how an independent consultant came to raise his rates seems to say that you must be so successful in your marketing that you find more work than you can handle, and so are forced to raise your rates and skim the cream at the top of the market. Some consultants believe that being able to charge such premium rates means that those consultants who do so are supersalesmen and -saleswomen. That is probably not true, or if it is, it is true only in a few cases. For the most part, consultants charging and getting such rates as $250 an hour are not spellbinders or in any way more persuasive sellers than most of us are. They are, however, self-confident, and they are completely convinced that they are worth what they charge. That is a firm requirement: You must believe that you are worth every penny of what you charge if you are to be successful in charging it. That is, you must set your own rates, according to your own beliefs of your worth and the worth of the services you perform for clients. Charging competitively is charging approximately what others charge. Think what that means: It means that you are letting others—your competitors and the $50 market that they have created—make your decisions and set your value and your rates. That consideration alone is ample reason to rethink how you set your rates.

> Setting your rates by what you think the market is for your services is letting others set your rates for you. Decide what *you* believe your services are worth, and let others decide for themselves what they think their services are worth.

PRICES AND MARKET/ CLIENT DEFINITION

A first step in rethinking how to set your rates is considering a few truths about markets and clients that may not have occurred to you before. One such truth is that you can classify markets and market niches in many ways, as you will learn later (in Chapter 7). One way is by prices. There are clients who would not buy a $20 gold piece if it were priced at 50 cents. They judge value by price, and will spurn the most qualified $50 consultant because he or she does not charge enough and so must not be very good. Of course, the reverse is true, and there are clients who will seek bids from a dozen or more consultants to find the lowest-priced one. That means, then, that there are $50 markets and there are $250 markets. Or there are $50 clients and there are $250 clients. In either case, you may decide for yourself which market/client you will pursue, for it is you who decides what is your market. You are not compelled to choose the $50 market and client.

It is harder to find and win $250 clients than to find and win $50 clients. On the other hand, one $250 client is worth five $50 clients. And the difference in benefits is more than money. It is also job satisfaction, peace of mind, greater pride in your work, and better client relations, to name several, as listed in the previous section.

If you ask for $250 as your rate, you must provide a $250 service. Even the client who normally evaluates a service by its price will not pay $250 for a $50 value. Be sure that your service is, indeed, what you demand for it.

> You can't charge $50 clients $250; you must pass up the $50 markets and clients and seek out the $250 markets and clients. Nor can you charge $250 and provide a $50 service. You must provide a service that is worth what you charge.

This not to say that you should immediately raise your rates five times over or that the $250 used as an example is the right target for you. You will have to evaluate the local market, if you wish to work in only the local market, or, conversely, how far and to where you must travel to find markets and clients who will pay whatever rates you have decided you must ask for. The right increase for you may be less than the example given or it may be greater. You will have to find out for yourself what works best for you. But it is almost certain that you are worth more than you think you are, and you're getting less than you are worth because you are limiting yourself. So do consider what *you* should be charging, what you and your services are worth, and never mind what others charge or think they are worth. Those opinions are self-fulfilling prophecies. You cannot be worth more than you think you are worth. A client is not going to believe what you do not believe. Moreover, the client who believes that price is an indicator of worth is going to be critical and expect your service to be worth what you charge for it.

AN ETHICAL PROBLEM IN HOURLY RATES

There is one factor in connection with hourly rates that is too often overlooked by both the consultant and the client. The factor is productivity. Let us suppose that you charge $75 per hour for your regular function of putting together a direct mail program to sell some kind of medium-priced commodity, while a competitor charges the same rate for the same kind of service. And let us assume that you and your competitor are approximately equal in experience and qualifications. Does one of you offer a greater value than the other?

On the face of it, it looks like a trade-off. But suppose that you happen to work a great deal faster than your competitor and can provide the desired service to the client in one-half the number of hours your competitor will require. The client will get a bargain when he or she hires you, and you will be working much too cheaply. Should you work cheaply because you are fast at what you do? There must be something wrong with that idea.

That involves more than one problem. There is, for one, the ethical problem. Should you slow down deliberately or should you give the client your best efforts, despite the fact that you will be grossly underpaid thereby? On the other hand, if you are the slower worker, the client pays more and perhaps is overpaying. You can see immediately that working on the basis of hourly rates, either you or the client may suffer.

There is also the problem of the client's perception of what your rate of production means, and what that does to your reputation. If you are naturally swift in your work, the client may interpret that as doing careless work, but if you are slow, the client may interpret that as taking forever to get a job done. Too, the use of an hourly rate tends to put you into the class of an employee, rather than of a contractor, in the client's view. That tends to make you appear, to a client, to be a subordinate, rather than an equal businessperson, reducing your negotiating effectiveness.

Suppose that you are not a naturally fast worker, but you have invested about $1,000 in some special equipment that doubles the rate at which you can get the job done. Must you pass all the savings on to the client, or are you entitled to recover your investment in that special equipment and profit from the investment by charging for the number of hours the job would have taken before you bought that equipment? After all, you made that investment to make more money in your business, did you not? But, again, there is that ethical problem of falsifying your accounts and charging for more hours than you actually worked.

One way to handle this is to talk with the prospect and explain these facts, under the assumption that the client needs the education and will see your point immediately. That does not mean that he or she will accept your higher rate or suggestion to contract for the work on a fixed-price contract basis. Neither does it mean that trying to educate the client and sell one of your suggested alternatives is a good idea or likely to be successful. Rather, the problem is probably best approached by explaining that it is in the client's best interests to accept a proposal and thus be able to review the consultant's reasoning and planning. Of course, you are suggesting only that the client accept an unsolicited proposal from you, but it is likely that the client will, if he or she buys your arguments, want to invite several consultants to submit proposals. That is a risk you will have to face and consider. (See the more detailed discussion of proposals in Chapter 8.)

That is an argument for preferring fixed-price projects, as well as an argument for charging higher rates than others. Take all these factors into consideration when deciding what your service is worth.

> Your productivity, the rate at which you produce the results your client wants, should be a major factor in what you charge for your service.

OTHER KINDS OF MARKET DEFINITIONS

This discussion has been focused on rates, usually hourly ones, although it can all be applied to setting a daily rate, if daily rates are more appropriate to what you do than are hourly rates. It has also been focused on the definition of clients and markets by their expectations in regard to rates charged by independent consultants. Earlier, we talked about the pros and cons of pricing your services by hourly or daily rates versus charging fixed prices to satisfy clients' needs as individual projects.

That is yet another basis for definition of markets and clients. There are clients who prefer to contract for hours or days of work and may not make exceptions and consider projects and fixed prices as a way to satisfy their needs. Or they may decide on an individual basis which is the more appropriate way to get a certain need satisfied. But there are also clients who contract only on a project basis at fixed prices. And so you may define markets and clients in this manner, as hourly/daily rates markets and clients and project/fixed-price markets and clients. Again, you may plan your marketing according to this consideration, for there are consultants who will accept only fixed-price projects, and there are others who will work on an hourly or daily basis only.

However you wish to view defining and choosing markets on this basis, your success depends partly on client expectations. If a client has a problem or need that he or she judges (perhaps even budgeted for) to be a $40,000 problem and you estimate to be a $25,000 problem, you run a serious risk of getting no consideration because you do not, in the client's opinion, understand the problem. On the other hand, if you estimate the project to be worth $75,000, you also run the risk of rejection without further consideration because your estimate is too far above the client's to give reasonable hope of negotiating an acceptable compromise. Again, you must somehow get an idea of what the client's perception is, regardless of what markets and clients you settle on as your marketing targets.

> You can decide to bid only for fixed-price projects, but you will have to find markets and clients for fixed-price projects, and you will still have to be sensitive to and responsive to client expectations.

Chapter

5

Using Lawyers, Accountants, and Other Special Services

You will probably require the help of other technical and professional specialists at least occasionally, so you need to know when and how to use their services wisely and in a way that best serves your business interests and preserves your control.

THE AGE OF THE SPECIALIST

We live in an era of specialization, largely the consequence of the growing expansion of knowledge in most areas; it has simply become impossible for the average practitioner in most fields to be the master of the entire field. It is not only sales specialists who have had to choose areas in which to excel. For example, there is no such entity as an engineer; an engineer is one of a given breed of engineers: We have mechanical engineers, electrical engineers, electronics engineers, rocket engineers, chemical engineers, stress engineers, computer engineers, civil engineers, aeronautical engineers, methods engineers, industrial engineers, and many other engineering classes and categories; the list goes on. But it does not stop there; within each special field there are subspecialties that develop as the field grows, and the trend is fated to continue, steadily creating even newer specialties.

Lawyers specialize, too—criminal lawyers, corporate lawyers, trial lawyers, divorce lawyers, medical-malpractice lawyers, tax lawyers, and others. Physicians have long specialized, and even the general practitioner is now a specialist, engaging in the specialty known as family practice, much of which is concerned with preliminary diagnosis and knowing what kinds of specialists to refer the patient to or call on for consultation. Even accountants specialize, as the variety of needs expands.

It is thus not surprising that we often find ourselves forced to turn to specialists for guidance, nor is there anything wrong in doing so. But there is a great deal that is wrong, quite often, in the ways we seek out such help and even more so in the ways we use that help.

> We consultants need to turn to consultants and experts on taxes, accounting, insurance, and other problems. The fees we pay them for help are ordinary business expenses and deductible as such.

DO YOU NEED A LAWYER?

We all have legal problems from time to time, and sometimes they are serious enough to require the services of a lawyer. In some cases, a letter to someone on a lawyer's letterhead works wonders. When I could get no response from a former employer who owed me a couple of months' salary, a letter from my attorney brought a prompt response, indicating a willingness to negotiate. And when I needed to know what the law was and how it would probably apply in a particular situation with which I was faced, I consulted my lawyer for his opinion and advice. For a problem out of his field, I've had to seek out or ask my lawyer to recommend another lawyer, one whose specialty covered my need of the moment.

I've always understood that what my lawyer advised was his opinion, based on his knowledge of the law, his experience as a lawyer, and his analysis of the information I had provided. (That latter often depended on how well he understood or failed to understand my business and my business problems.) I was particularly aware that what my lawyer offered was opinion—*his* opinion—not final judgment from on high.

That is not an insignificant consideration. Quite the contrary, it is one major point of this entire chapter: The experts you consult—lawyers, accountants, engineers, computer specialists, and consultants of various stamps and breeds—offer their judgments and opinions, and we hope that they offer reasoned, objective, and wise recommendations. But these are, at best, only recommendations, not the decisions that must be made; only you can make those final decisions. Do not expect nor permit those specialists to make your decisions for you, although some will be trying to do just that in their enthusiasm and desire to help. Despite their education and experience, they can be wrong. In any case, decision making concerning your venture is your responsibility always. You cannot escape it, and no one should be allowed to usurp it, not even accidentally or unconsciously.

Take the simple case of your question as to whether you ought to incorporate. You put the question to your lawyer. Can he or she give you a truly objective answer? It is difficult to do so because arranging your incorporation for you probably means a fee of $1,000 or more to your lawyer for a relatively simple and routine set of services.

Experts offer opinions and recommendations. They do not—should not be permitted to—make your business decisions. Only you should do that. Weigh what the expert tells you, and then make your decision.

You need to know what to ask for when you seek expert help. How does your lawyer know whether incorporation is a good idea for you? Does he or she understand your business? Your lawyer is a legal adviser, not a business or management adviser, and does not understand your business and your business needs. Instead of asking your lawyer for his or her judgment or recommendation, ask for facts. What a lawyer can and should tell you—should be asked—is what incorporation costs and what it means; for example:

✔ What is the initial cost?

✔ What are the secondary costs (e.g., additional accounting and other reports and paperwork)?

✔ What new taxes will a corporation have to support?

✔ What are the benefits (if any)?

✔ What are the alternatives (e.g., less costly and less difficult ways of accomplishing the same ends)?

> Think carefully when you turn to an expert for help about what you really want to—*need to*—know. Be sure to ask the right questions and insist on answers that you can understand.

Armed with answers to these and perhaps other, related questions, you are in a position to ponder the advisability of incorporating. It is easy enough and cheap enough to become incorporated, but perhaps you would only open a Pandora's box of issues and costs that force you to throw money at problems resulting from the act of incorporating.

Most experienced lawyers understand these principles quite well, and will not attempt to force their judgments on you or make your decisions for you. They will usually try to present a balanced view—the alternatives available to you and the pros and cons of each—and ask you to express an opinion; or, at most, they will offer a recommendation even if it is not specifically asked for. But there are others who, in their eagerness to serve, will attempt to force their opinions on you to invoke a decision they champion. It is up to you to see that this is not permitted to happen.

IS IT ALL OVER YOUR HEAD?

We all get a little confused, awed, and even intimidated by the special jargon of lawyers, accountants, engineers, and others, and we suspect that perhaps they deliberately use that jargon as a defensive measure to perpetuate their mastery and dominance. We sense, sometimes, that they seem to be saying to us, "You wouldn't understand, so take my word for it."

I reject that, and so should you. It is my opinion that every specialist you retain to help you in some way is obligated to make clear verbal or written reports justifying his or her actions and bills. Most important, that other specialist is obligated to explain what he or she has done or proposes to do, what action he or she recommends, and why he or she recommends that action. I believe that I am capable of understanding every situation, in principle at least, and that it is the obligation of any specialist I hire to explain matters to me in language I can understand. I insist on that, and you should also: Understanding is what you are paying for, and recommendations are of little value to you if you do not fully understand the rationale for them so that you can judge them for yourself and make your decisions on the basis of what you understand and not on blind faith in someone's opinion.

The Case of the Accountant

What has been said here about using lawyers' services well applies equally to other specialists you turn to occasionally. Perhaps the most difficult professional for us ordinary people to understand is the accountant. Consider the kinds of minds that have developed the forms, manipulations, and instructions necessary to prepare even a simple tax return! The tax laws grow more and more complex, while we are being assured that they are being simplified, and we grow more and more reliant on accountants to keep our books and prepare our tax returns, especially when we are in a business venture and must cope with such added complications as assets, liabilities, depreciation, amortization, and other mysterious terms that trip so easily from the accountant's lips but which our lips are reluctant to utter because we are not at all sure what they mean. But let us try to get a better understanding of why we must keep accounts and what we ought to do with the record—what, in fact, accounting is. (It is true that a great many people in business, small and large, do not understand what accounting is; but my seminar experience proved clearly to me that many are eager to learn more about it if it can be explained in simple language.)

Many people believe that we are required to maintain accounting systems for the convenience of the IRS. It is easy to understand how such a notion has gained currency, for we do have to have records to substantiate our tax returns and claims made therein. An accountant who understands the tax laws can save us many dollars each year, so our accounting systems ought to be designed to maximize the tax benefits possible. Even so, beneficial though it is, that is not the prime reason for the existence of a formal accounting system. The prime purpose of the accounting system is to help us manage our business affairs successfully. Specifically, it is to provide feedback—information—on which to base our management decisions. It must help us in detecting unwarranted expenses, determining what operations are profitable and which are not, and other concerns. The system ought to generate reports for that purpose, and large systems do. In the small system, such as you and I normally use, we can usually get our information directly from the books by scanning them frequently. And that is one of the problems in turning your books over to a public accountant—at least some of the public accountants I have met and turned my books over to: Either they have your books in their offices most of the time or they visit you to make postings only once a week or once every two weeks. So the information you get is history and not current events; it is therefore not of much use in managing your venture.

The Communication Difficulty

I think it quite possible that accountants and other specialists are so accustomed to thinking only in terms of their own jargon that they become quite incapable of thinking of their own work in simple English; much less can they translate it for others. Take the simple term "cost of sales," for example; what does it mean? You or I might ordinarily assume that cost of sales refers to the cost of marketing, the cost of making sales or winning the orders. That is a reasonable inference, and it is a figure that is of considerable use to a manager. But that is not what the term means to an accountant. The accountant regards the term as including all costs incurred for or by an item before it is sold.

Beware of applying everyday-language definitions to accounting terms or other professional jargon; standard dictionaries are not reliable indicators of meaning in this special world. Take the apparently simple distinction of running your business on a "cash basis." To laypeople, that means "no tickee no shirtee" or payment up front, cash on delivery, and in some businesses it even means that only currency is accepted—no checks or charges. But to an accountant a cash basis system means you post a receipt, a record of income, when a payment check arrives, and you post a debit when you pay a bill. The alternative system is to post a receipt as income when you send out an invoice to a customer and make that bill a receivable, and you post a debit when you receive a bill and make that bill a payable.

In light of all this, it is easy to understand the difficulty of communication with an accountant. So you must learn the language of accounting, at least at a beginner's level, along with the basic principles or concepts. You must then compel the accountant to explain him- or herself in simple English. The alternative would be to abandon all efforts to probe the mysteries of accounting, and simply accept what your accountant does and says, with crossed fingers and silent prayers that your accountant is an honest and wise one.

Certainly, you ought to reject that last option, as it represents too many hazards; you almost surely underestimate the importance of accounting to the success of your venture if you are willing to do that. The option of learning at least the rudiments and jargon of accounting may be little more than hope, for many accountants, I have found, have great difficulty translating their jargon into understandable everyday prose. The best option is probably to press your accountant for precise explanations, and to apply some of that ordinary wisdom we refer to as common sense. (Surely you are as bright as your accountant, despite his or her special education in that career field.) For example, pressed by my accountant for a decision on the cost estimates in a proposal that had been offered to me, I demurred because I was skeptical of the costs presented; I thought the risk of loss on my side rather excessive. But the accountant, working with the executive who had prepared the proposal, offered me a rather elaborate presentation of his own cost analysis, showing a favorable bottom line, or so he alleged.

Lacking financial and accounting expertise, I was unable to understand and appreciate this sophisticated presentation, and so was forced to either accept it or find a means to analyze it. I therefore resorted to an expedient that would have been far too simple for any professional accountant to put to use, and used that expedient to analyze the figures on the simplest profit-loss revelation I could devise: I drew a line down the center of a blank sheet and headed the two columns thus created as shown in Figure 5.1.

FIGURE 5.1 Simple method for analyzing costs and profits.

Dollars Out	Dollars In
Totals:	

I then asked that each of the numbers in the presentation be transferred to the appropriate column, after which I added each column and compared the totals. The individual in question was no longer able to support an argument for profitability of the contract in question when the chart showed dollars going out exceeding dollars coming in. The obvious moral of this little tale: Always try to simplify analyses and presentations as the most reliable way of determining what is fact.

I am sure that the accountant was sincere in offering me his cost and profit analysis, and that is perhaps the danger in abandoning our basic human judgment and replacing it with elaborate procedures: It is easy to practice an unconscious self-deceit when relying on obscure and complex methodology that you do not completely grasp. Be suspicious of anything you do not fully understand.

BEWARE OF READY-MADE SOLUTIONS AND CONVENTIONAL WISDOM

Sometimes the experts you turn to attempt to impose their favorite preconceived ideas on you, basing their urgent recommendations on their authority as experts. Be wary of experts with favorite formulas for success, ready-made solutions to your problems, and other patent or improvised ideas about how to conduct your business. (You may occasionally hear of this kind of thing as a solution looking for a matching problem.) Well-intentioned though many of these experts are, they often tend, perhaps unconsciously, to try to force fit you to their own notions of how your business ought to be run. (My own accountant periodically attempts to interpose himself as my business manager, suggesting how much I ought to charge clients and what services I should sell, and otherwise advising me in business matters about a business with which he is not at all familiar.)

> Remember always that consulting is a custom service. Each requirement has its unique conditions, and calls for a unique response, one designed specifically for the case. Beware always of off-the-shelf solutions, whether you are the consultant or the client. Such solutions are rarely good fits, unless modified to be an exact fit.

One of the hazards presented by consultation with many experts is their advocacy of conventional wisdom, for there is a body of conventional wisdom surrounding every business and profession. For example, some of those advising me on the mail order business years ago explained the conventional wisdom of that field, as they understood it, including the following, among other choice morsels of marketing knowledge that were all but guaranteed to keep me out of trouble and bring me early success:

- ✔ Summer months, June through August, are dreadfully slow, and it is a waste of money to do any marketing in those months.
- ✔ Business will pick up briskly after Labor Day, and remain good until spring.
- ✔ Printing sales literature in several colors improves results.
- ✔ Printing sales literature on a more expensive grade of paper will produce better results.
- ✔ A postage-paid return envelope enclosed with the sales literature will greatly increase the number of orders returning.

Are these all myths? No, they are not myths in that they are based on truths, and there is usually a seed (a tiny seed) of truth buried therein. But they are not reliable rules, either. They are partial truths, true under certain circumstances or true occasionally and untrue at other times. The improvement in response due to multicolor printing and/or postage-paid response envelopes is so slight, in percentage terms, that a significant increase in income (if any) is apparent only when the mailing is very large. Postage-paid response envelopes help to some degree when you are mailing to individuals, but are of negligible influence when you mail to businesses, I have found. And I could find no evidence that spending more money for a better grade of paper improved results. So, true or not, the myths had no significance for me.

And yet, despite this, I do not discount the advice, for something prompted those beliefs, and that something was probably that observing them appeared to make a difference in some cases. The problem is that it is not possible to predict with any certainty in which cases these tips will prove to be helpful, but only that they will be valid for occasional situations.

INHERENT PARADOX OF CONVENTIONAL WISDOM

As a matter of course in all fields, a few of those with experience present themselves as experts and offer advice and pat answers that are not total untruths, and yet are often highly misleading. Every field has its burden of conventional wisdom. But in this ever more dynamic era, where change is the most predictable element, conventional wisdom has this inherent paradox: It tends to have a short life and be obsolescent by the time it becomes conventional wisdom! That is, it is often a collection of yesterday's truths with little relevance to today's rapidly changing world.

The best use of conventional wisdom is to accept it as a working premise, tentatively only, before committing your resources to it. Do not reject it totally, for it does represent someone's successful experience and knowledge, but do not accept it as applicable to your situation and use without testing its validity for you and your situation. In fact, treat all expert advice with that kind of caution, for even the general truth is valid only for an assumed set of circumstances and conditions, and is rarely if ever universally true. On one occasion when someone advised me that an advertising piece I had designed was dreadful and inevitably destined for failure, I was dismayed because I had already had a large quantity printed. Reluctant to discard that printing and waste the money, I invested enough additional money to make a test mailing. To my delight, the mailing was highly successful, and I mailed the rest of the new literature in a successful follow-up campaign. That does not mean that my adviser of that moment was incompetent, but only that he was too sure that his assessment was correct for me and my situation of the moment. Another time, in another promotion, that sales piece might well have been a complete loser.

> Be wary of conventional wisdom. It may be yesterday's truth, but is it today's truth? Use healthy skepticism and common sense.

The lesson is really that there are no sure things. Even an exact duplicate of a prior success does not ensure another success. There are imponderables in most situations—factors and influences—some of them pure chance, but all almost impossible to foresee.

CAN YOU DO IT YOURSELF?

Although you should not hesitate to turn to another consultant or specialist when you need help, there are many things you can do for yourself. There may be important benefits, other than saving money, in doing so.

With all of the increasing vertical specialization in these times, there is still a strong do-it-yourself thread running through our society. This is not only with respect to assembling a TV stand, repairing a leaky faucet, or paneling your basement, however. Specialists of all kinds prepare do-it-yourself guides for the rest of us, and you may wish to consider doing that yourself a bit later on. We have already mentioned that you can handle your own incorporation or registration of a fictitious (d/b/a) name for your venture, and you can buy a ready-made corporate kit of bylaws, forms, stock certificates, and seal. Too, even a casual survey of bookstore shelves will reveal books offering to guide you as a layperson in handling your own divorce suit or bankruptcy, writing contracts, dealing with bank officials (see Chapter 7), managing your investment portfolio, and providing forms to help you file official documents properly. A visit to any large business supplies retail store will turn up a wealth of do-it-yourself aids in books, ready-made forms, computer programs, and other such items. You can now publish your own newsletter and do a great many other things that were once the exclusive province of the specialist. The desktop computer, with the flood of software that has become available, is no small factor in making it possible to do it yourself. (For example, I personally rely little on printeries and copy shops now, since I can easily print my own labels, forms, brochures, and other printed items I use in small quantities.)

This leads to an inevitable problem of trying to decide what you can and should do for yourself versus what you should entrust only to the hands of an experienced professional. It is no small problem. Most of us have an almost childlike faith in the expert specialist. A physician, especially one who looks the part and has a charismatic manner, is no less than a god. We are awed by the self-confident lawyer who comforts and reassures us when we are worried about some problem with the authorities. We are even impressed by the TV service technician who obviously truly understands the magic of picking pictures out of thin air and can get that ailing set doing so again. What we need to assess accurately is what we can do for ourselves effectively and what is more efficiently done for us by someone else. Your judgment is involved here.

> There are many things you can do for yourself, but doing them yourself is not always the wisest move. Weigh the amount of skill and knowledge required, the cost in time against your work schedule and commitments, and the risk before deciding.

Perhaps we have a need for a bit of awe and faith, finding comfort in it. And perhaps it is justified in certain individual cases. But I am often mindful of the preface to a textbook on calculus, in which the author urged the reader to lose any awe or fear of the subject. "What one fool has learned, another fool can learn," the author argued. And that is true for all fields. Obviously, you cannot take out your own gallbladder, nor should you argue your own case in court, but always bear in mind that the specialist is a fallible human being, too, despite his or her specialized knowledge, training, and experience. You can do for yourself many of the things a specialist can advise you on or do for you, as in the case of establishing a simple close corporation or registering a fictitious (d/b/a) business name, discussed earlier. Not all the things the specialists do require years of training and experience; many require only normal intelligence and readily available guidance.

But the issue is not always whether you *can* do some of the specialized functions yourself; there is the question of whether you *should* do some of these things yourself, whether there are considerations other than the economy of doing it for yourself. Let's take the case of the accounting function.

YOUR FRIEND, THE ACCOUNTANT

The firm of H&R Block has become a large and highly successful corporation, almost an institution, by providing a relatively simple service, still known best for its original simple service of preparing tax returns for individuals. This service continues to be the main subject of its advertising, although H&R Block is today a large conglomerate corporation, encompassing a number of companies.

By far the majority of all tax preparers' customers could make out their own tax returns, although many claim an inability to do so. They are mystified by the bureaucratic language and structure of the forms, and awed by the mental gymnastics required to translate the cryptic

IRS instructions into practice. They have a rather complete lack of faith in their own ability to do the job. Moreover, it is far more convenient to have a specialist prepare the return, and so millions go to professional tax preparers for what is really a simple job.

Convenience alone is powerful motivator, but many professional tax preparers are not reluctant to add motivation by encouraging fear of the complicated forms and possible audit. Nor do they shrink from using fear motivation to point out that those who prepare their own returns often fail to take advantage of all exemptions and deductions to which they are entitled, and thus may overpay their taxes and fail to get refunds.

A great many individuals who undertake a business venture also have a fear of attempting their own accounting in general. Many of us cringe at the idea of tackling anything even remotely connected with mathematics, and we are further intimidated by the jargon of the accounting professionals. Even when accountants use terms we think we understand, such as "cash basis," to refer to the accounting system, we often find ultimately that the term does not mean what we think it means.

Probably you can find several ready-made accounting systems that will serve your needs; most provide ample flexibility to satisfy individual requirements. However, you may believe that your venture is so specialized or so different that no *proprietary*, off-the-shelf accounting system will do for you. You can still handle your own postings: Any good accountant will set up a custom-designed system for you and instruct you in posting it, if you wish to do this yourself. (In fact, some accountants prefer this and will suggest it to you.)

proprietary
of ownership or owned by, as in proprietary information.

Of course, in today's world you need not do any of this manually. There are small accounting systems that will run easily on most desktop computers. You enter items via a keyboard, rather than a pen, and the program does the calculations and postings for you. There are also accounting programs that will calculate your taxes.

In short, it is no longer necessary to be an accountant or even a bookkeeper to keep your own accounts;

you don't even have to know how to calculate percentages or subtract line 4c from line 4b. You have many easily available practical options and alternatives to the traditional methods. You *can* do it yourself, if you wish to. But aside from whether you can or cannot do it yourself or whether you should or should not do it yourself, what is best for your business? Weigh the pros and cons and make your decision.

Chapter

Building a Clientele: Marketing

Building a consulting practice of any kind poses special problems and requires a different marketing approach, as is required to build most kinds of professional practices.

WHAT IS MARKETING?

Defining marketing succinctly and yet accurately is no easier than defining consulting. Technically, marketing is not the same as sales, despite the common use of the two terms as interchangeable ones. Still, we are really concerned here only with the end goal of marketing: to make sales or, as management guru Peter Drucker has put it, to create customers. Or, to relate the goal more closely with the milieu of the independent consultant, to win clients.

> The ultimate goal of marketing is sales or, in this case, winning clients, so focus on that (rather than on technical differences) as the meaning and objective of marketing your independent consulting services.

WINNING CLIENTS

It is not easy to persuade prospective clients to entrust you with what are important projects to them, especially when you are a complete stranger. That is at least part of the reason that conventional advertising does not work very well in winning clients. The most successful marketing approach for most consultants depends on building a personal professional image, for most independent consultants find that they depend on recommendations and referrals in a kind of word-of-mouth sales promotion to win clients. Those new to consulting who rely on conventional advertising, such as print, broadcast, and direct mail, almost invariably find that these bring little result. Prospective clients for consulting services are usually investing more than money in retaining a consultant. They are often undertaking serious business risk. The client who retains me to turn out a proposal risks both the cost of the proposal and the reputation that will result from the impression made by the proposal on his or her client. The client retaining you as a sales consultant is also undertaking a risk and usually a considerable cost in dollars.

It is not hard to understand why retaining you as a consultant usually represents a serious commitment by your client, who is going to want more than an advertisement or brochure as evidence that you are competent, ethical, and reliable. It is not a great deal different than when you are seeking a good allergist: You are likely to ask friends and relatives for recommendations, seeking an allergist with an established reputation. The most effective marketing approach for an independent consultant has proved to be that of building a reputation as able and trustworthy. That reputation, once earned, is itself a recommendation. Every time a prospective client reads or hears something that reports such a reputation, it is an endorsement by others, by popular opinion, just as though a friend or associate has personally recommended you to the prospective client.

> Your reputation as a practicing professional is the main key to winning clients, and your marketing success is in some direct proportion to the quality of that reputation and number of people who know you or know of you (i.e., know your reputation) whether they know you personally or not.

AN INTERESTING PHENOMENON

It is not unusual for satisfied clients and others who know you personally to recommend you and your services to others. Interestingly enough, however, strangers who know only of you will also often recommend you to others as though they knew you personally. So the achievement of referrals and recommendations via word-of-mouth channels need not depend on friends, relatives, or former clients; it can depend entirely on your visibility and image.

> Prospects who see or hear from you frequently and learn a great deal about you come to think of you as someone they know personally. Oddly enough, many of them will recommend you to others as though they are acquainted with your competence and trustworthiness from personal experience.

YOUR VISIBILITY

Visibility, as used here, refers to how widely and how well you and what you offer to do for others (i.e., clients) are known. The objective overall is to be visible to the maximum you can manage. A note here, however: It has not yet been stated, but it should be implicit that visibility is

 visibility the degree to which you are known as a consultant specialist.

useful only to the extent that it is visibility to the right audience (i.e., those who are prospective clients). It does no good to become highly visible to anyone who would never be likely to need or want your services.

Of course, no audience you reach is going to be composed 100 percent of prospects for your services, but you do want to be sure that the audience is predominantly one of good prospects, with at least a majority of it prospective clients.

> The benefit of a high degree of visibility depends on the suitability of the audience. Be sure that your audience is one in which a large proportion are individuals who are likely to have need for such services as you offer.

YOUR IMAGE

"Image" refers to how others perceive you. Ideally, as the basic characteristics of their impression, you want to project an image of a thoroughly competent and trustworthy independent consultant. There will be other characteristics that will help greatly to induce prospective clients to become actual clients. You will want to appear businesslike and yet friendly, one who is thoroughly professional and yet is truly interested in your clients and cares about their welfare and satisfaction. You want to be professional and businesslike, and yet one who will always take the time to answer questions and explain what you are doing and why you are doing it.

Image making should not be left to chance, to the possibility or probability that the prospect will deduce that your image includes those desirable characteristics. You must be aware of what you wish the prospect to perceive as your characteristics and take measures to influence the prospect accordingly. This effort is known in some advertising industry circles as "positioning." That refers to positioning yourself (your image) in the prospect's mind. Clients will learn to see you as one thing or another, relative to their own wants and needs. It's easy to convey an impression other than the one you want, such as becoming known as a copywriter when you really want to be seen as a campaign designer and manager.

> Be sure you know what image you wish prospects to have of you, and take steps to help prospects gain that image. Otherwise, you may wind up being offered other assignments than the kind you want and being passed up for the ones you want.

WHAT IS YOUR BUSINESS?

"What is your business?" is another way of asking, "What image do you want to have?" If you do not see parallelism now, read on. I hope you will see it shortly, as we examine this.

Everyone knows, or thinks he or she knows, what he or she is selling. I have conducted many tests of this idea at seminars, training courses, and other lecture sessions, sometimes even issuing a challenge by predicting that none of the listeners know what business they are in. I then invite all to tell me what their business is. The answers are always enlightening: Almost invariably the individual explains his or her own view of what he or she sells: consulting services, computers, office supplies, construction materials, building design, printing, graphic arts services, computer programming, and electronics engineering, among many other such definitions.

If I go on to ask why their clients and customers buy from them and not from their competitors, there is usually a prolonged silence. They don't know and they are waiting for me to speak, suspecting that my question is a loaded one. It is indeed loaded, for I want to make what I believe to be a most important point. The answer, in each case, if and when we can find it together, is the real secret of marketing success. It is what business is all about. It is why one business starts at a kitchen table and grows into a multimillion-dollar corporation, while another remains a kitchen-table enterprise forevermore.

Whose Wants Must Be Satisfied?

The problem is simple enough in principle: It is the problem (the mistake) of focusing on what we want rather than on what the customer wants—on what we want to sell (and think we are selling) rather than on what the customer wants to buy (and thinks he or she is buying).

Let us put this yet another way: When you are the customer do you concern yourself with what the seller wants or with what you want? That is, what do those who have become your clients see in you, and why did they become your clients? What is the image that induced them to want your help?

What many consultants and others in business find most difficult is fathoming what it is that the customer really wants, especially when the customer cannot always put it into words to define it. The late Charles Revson, founder of the Revlon cosmetics firm, understood the concept well and knew how to express it. Here is how he put it: "In the factory we make cosmetics; in the stores we sell hope." Thus one does not sell lipstick, rouge, mascara, perfume, and other such preparations; one sells beauty, stylishness, sex, romance, the illusion of a femme fatale.

In my own case, as a proposal consultant, my business was not helping clients write winning proposals (although that was my goal); it was helping my clients win contracts. That was the real result they wanted, what they would pay for.

My own motivation as a client was no different. I bought my computers from Paul, who built them and charged top prices for his product. I paid those prices because I thought them a bargain in view of the superb nature of his support of sales. Never was there the slightest argument about any service I required when something did not work right. Never was there the slightest hesitation to make any adjustment or repair I requested, nor any hesitancy to explain something to me or give me advice when I needed it. And Paul took the trouble to understand how I used my computer so he could always advise me well on what equipment was best for my needs.

In short, he did not see his business as building and selling computers, but as helping his customers have the right equipment for their needs and enjoy trouble-free service. In the days when IBM dominated the computer market with its behemoth mainframes, it was commonly accepted that customers bought IBM computers because IBM provided superb service. The average customer did not really care whether the IBM computer was technically superior or inferior to others; the customer wanted reliable and trouble-free computer operation, and that is what IBM's service provided. A computer that rarely broke down was still a problem if the customer had to wait days for a service technician to call and make repairs. A system that broke down frequently but was supplied by a company that always had a service technician working on the computer to get it back in operation the same day was effectively much more reliable.

In short, you sell the benefit. It is providing the chief benefit that induces the prospect to buy that is your business. So, as a sales consultant, your business is not writing a powerful direct mail package, designing a killer sales promotion, or improving the sales skills and performances of the client's sales staff; it is creating sales for your client, whether that is sales in the client's regular line, a new line, or a new medium.

You can't define your business or shape your image effectively from the view on your side of the seller-buyer interface. You can do so only from the view on the buyer's side of the interface, identifying what your satisfied clients see you as that induces them to be your clients.

The Key Question

In talking with prospective clients, whether that is face-to-face in their offices, from a lecture platform, within an e-mail discussion group, or under any other circumstances, the important thing is to listen, rather than to talk, for you are—or should be—looking for information. The key question to which you are seeking an answer is, "How can I make you my client?" No one is better qualified to provide the answer you want than is the prospect. And yet, the prospect probably could not answer that question if you asked it directly.

The question a client could answer, if asked directly, is, "What are your most pressing problems right now?" (Or, as independent consultant Peter Meyer puts it, "What keeps you up at night?"

The point here is that consulting is helping clients solve problems and satisfy needs via custom solutions and services. The seller of a product can sell only the features and benefits that are inherent in that product, but you are selling services that you will design specifically to satisfy the client's needs—although you must first know what those needs are, and which are most important to the prospect.

It would probably be a great mistake to ask that question bluntly, especially to a prospective client to whom you are still a total stranger. You must approach it more discreetly by asking general questions and then giving the prospect ample time to respond. Ask the prospect to tell you about his or her business, or the work handled, in the case of an employee. Then sit back and listen, speaking briefly only to answer a question from the prospect or to ask another question designed to keep the information flowing. If you listen carefully and interpose new questions only to guide and stimulate the information flow, you will get the answers you need: You will learn what problems and needs trouble the prospect, and you will be able to distinguish those that are most important to the prospect and most suitable for addressing with the services you offer.

Make it a prime objective of your marketing to learn as much as possible about your prospects' needs and problems if you want to target your sales appeals most effectively. Don't approach or engage prospects in conversation to talk (i.e., to make sales presentations); engage prospects in conversation to listen, to learn how to make them clients. Only then is it time for you to talk, to explain how you can help the prospect solve problems and satisfy needs through your services.

> You don't learn a prospect's needs by talking. You learn them by listening. Never visit prospects to tell them about yourself and your services. Visit them to learn about them and what they do.

PROMISE AND PROOF

Yet another way to view this is to look at all advertising and selling as based on two major functions, promise and proof. First you make a promise, a promise to deliver a certain benefit, and then you present the needed proof to satisfy the prospect that your promise is valid and reliable. That is, you first project your image, position yourself, and define your business as help in winning/increasing sales volume. That is a promise, and it is easy to make, but prospective clients know that and they are not naive, so they want some proof that you can and will do what you promise. Hence you need to follow up the promise with some evidence, such as names of clients for whom you have done what you promise, what it is that you did for them, testimonials, your credentials in general, and/or whatever else you believe will be convincing proof of your competence and reliability to do what you promise. All successful selling can be shown to be just that, regardless of embellishments.

> All selling is promise—the end benefit your client will receive—and proof that you can and will keep that promise and deliver that benefit. That is what the prospect buys in becoming your client.

HOW TO BUILD THAT VISIBILITY AND IMAGE

You've read here that conventional advertising and promotion—print advertising and broadcast commercials, brochures, direct mail, and others—do not work well in selling consulting services, and never have. What has worked in various forms has been a process generally called *networking*, a particularly appropriate term today, as you shall see. One convenient and readily available medium for doing so is that of e-mail as a medium for open discussion groups.

DISCUSSION GROUPS

There are many, many e-mail–based discussion groups—sometimes referred to as mailing lists—based on some subject of common interest, very much like the electronic bulletin boards that arose before the Internet. There is one, for example, for authors of computer books, another for cancer victims, another for consultants. Overall, the number is quite great, mounting into the thousands.

These are useful for making yourself known and developing your reputation as a consultant. Of course, you want to select a group of individuals who appear to be good prospects for what you do, and you must be active in the discussions. You may belong to a group of independent consultants for purposes of keeping up with what consultants are doing, and it is possible that you may even get an occasional client by referral through

networking
creating a network; raising your visibility and enhancing your professional image through activities aimed to do these things, such as word-of-mouth advertising and publicity.

your activities with the group. However, that group is not a prime marketing ground for you, unless your specialty is helping other consultants win clients. Whatever groups you do select are estimates, guesses. Test them and drop those that do not produce results for you. Experience will soon tell you how well you have estimated.

> Be sure to seek out and join one or more discussion groups of those who appear most likely to be good prospects for your services. Be active in the group so that all get to know you and what you do for clients.

NETWORKING

The networking concept is a simple one: It is developing a wide circle of friends and acquaintances who know of your professional abilities and have good things to say to others about you in that respect. With networking done well, prospective clients learn enough about you so that you are no longer a total stranger to them, but someone they know almost personally and come to trust as a reliable and able professional. That objective is, of course, a prime one.

Traditionally, making oneself well known and building a favorable reputation within a *network* was and is the reason many entrepreneurs joined and were active in business clubs, fraternal organizations, and business and professional associations of various kinds. It was and is also why they attend as many conventions, trade shows, and other such events as possible. These are the well-established, classic methods of networking—meeting those who are potential clients and possible contacts with potential clients. The popularity of that basis for networking has declined somewhat today, with the much greater

 network the string of friends, acquaintances, and others you develop who know you and of you, and pass the word along to others.

efficiency and much wider grasp now possible via Internet connections. The fact is that today your network need not be confined to those you count as friends and personal acquaintances. Your network now can and should include a great many others, those who only know of you or become directly acquainted with you through online discussion groups, electronic newsletters and magazines, and other modern avenues of communication. In fact, as you read earlier, you will be surprised at how many who know of you only by reputation or by reading your messages will recommend you to others on the strength of that impression.

Networking is the key to building your professional image and raising your visibility. Devote at least part of your time to building and maintaining your network, for it must be maintained or it will gradually evaporate.

Today we rely far less on personal activity in associations and related events and much more on cyberspace communications opportunities (the Internet, primarily) via e-mail, chat rooms, web sites, and other such activities. It is possible to do most or even all of your networking through these media, forming friendships with many people you never meet face-to-face, and building a wide reputation that brings you new clients. Of course, you can do a great deal more networking in this manner, working from your own desk and reaching far greater numbers of people than you can reach by physically joining groups of people at such activities as listed earlier.

One way to do this effectively is to join e-mail discussion groups and participate as actively as possible, making yourself known as a knowledgeable professional who has answers for sales problems and the capability to provide clients with whatever sales support services you offer as your specialties. You can also create your own electronic newsletter, special reports, and other products that help you build your reputation and make you visible to a great many others. Be sure that you make it known that you are a professional consultant, always in quest of new clients, and remind everyone of that frequently. Never assume that others already know that you are an independent consultant or that they remember that fact.

> Make cyberspace a principal means for networking by becoming active as a busy participant in cyberspace arenas that have relevance to sales activities and those who are potential clients and contacts.

Network Maintenance

Be aware that your network is perishable, as are all things, and must be maintained. No matter how well known you become or how great a reputation you acquire, people will forget you quickly enough if you begin to drop from sight. Unless your practice, of itself, produces all the recommendations and referrals you can handle, you cannot afford to relax your networking efforts. *Network maintenance* should be a permanent or at least long-term part of your marketing program—and perhaps all of it, under some circumstances.

The Effect of Writing Well

Much of my own success in networking was due in large part to my being a professional writer and doing that— writing—quite well after so many years of practice and experience. Normally, members of a discussion group send their posts to the group for all to read. However, to this day, strangers often address me directly and personally with letters because they have found something I've written to the group as part of a typical online discussion

 **network maintenance** continuous activity to keep your visibility high and your image what you want it to be by reminders and replacement of losses in network.

to be of special interest to them. They may have found some facts I offered interesting, or they may have been intrigued by my orientation and views in relation to a discussion of some subject.

The final chapter of this book discusses writing itself and presents views on how to write well, but for now there is one point that I think is important to make about writing: "Writing well" does not refer only to fluency or eloquence in using the language, because writing well is thinking well. Extremely few of us, even among professional writers, write good first drafts because in a first draft we have usually not yet thought out how to organize and present our views. In fact, I, like many other writers, deliberately use my first draft of any writing to help me think the subject out. (I have heard this referred to as "thinking on paper," which to me is an apt description.) But not only have we not thought out how to present our views yet, but too often we have not even thought out what our views are! You need to know just what you really think about a subject to write well about it, and rewriting your early drafts helps you think the subject out. I therefore usually try to write my e-mail posts to groups as carefully as I write something for formal publication. It helps me think a subject out when I see my first ideas marching across the page.

KEEP YOUR EYE ON THE BALL

Never lose sight of your ultimate goal in all of this networking activity: You are in quest of clients and contracts. Still, you must attend to your more immediate objective in becoming visible and building an image. Marketing is no place for modesty. You must always work earnestly at proving that you are knowledgeable and capable. You can do this without offensive bragging through the way in which you respond to others, always remembering that you are being judged by what you have to say and your effectiveness in saying it diplomatically.

You may hear from other consultants advice to be close-mouthed in offering information in these activities. Some consultants believe that they must guard against giving away any advice or information unless the other party is paying for it. That is a shortsighted view in my opinion. Without providing samples of your expert knowledge and sound judgment, how will you build a reputation? Of course, all you will be giving away are samples of your consulting services. Those represent an important sales tool.

> Be free with samples of your knowledge and capability. They are a first and most effective means of demonstrating what you can do for a client, and should be used to whet the appetites of prospective clients.

EVERY BUSINESS IS A SERVICE BUSINESS

The point has been made by some marketing experts that every business is a service business, even those that sell common commodities, such as shoes and shaving cream. The point made by that assertion is this: Customers buy products for what the product *does* for the customer. One buys a large automobile because he or she has a large family or for some other reason needs (or believes he or she needs) a large automobile, rather than a small one. Or perhaps one buys the most expensive model of some product because "most expensive" is equated by the customer with "best," and he or she wants the comfort of believing he or she bought the best. And so the argument is that customers do not want the product for its own sake, but for what the customer believes the product will do. That brings up the question of what you really are selling (or ought to be selling).

WHAT ARE YOU REALLY SELLING?

Marketing principles do not change, regardless of the marketing media and targets. Their basis is the art of persuasion, and that is the art of presenting the most attractive benefits of buying what you offer.

Every proper sales presentation is an offer, not an announcement. An offer isn't just a description of what you propose to sell, an announcement. For example, "HUGE JULY 4TH SALE!" is merely an announcement, not an offer. "SAVE 22% TO 27% AT JULY 4TH SALE!" is an offer. It is what you offer to *do* for the prospect. It is the promise of a benefit that you hope will motivate the prospect to become your client.

Note that distinction: An offer is a promise, a promise of some important benefit the client will gain as a result of buying your service. What you sell is a promise because it can't be anything else at this point, before you deliver your service.

> Your true offer is always a promise, a promise to deliver to the client some powerfully persuasive benefit, a reward for buying what you sell. The offer itself must motivate, as a first step.

THE PROMISE IS NOT ENOUGH

We live in a sophisticated age. Almost everyone has become far more sophisticated in this era of world travel, television, computers, and the Internet. Very few of the public will buy snake oil and smug assurances today. The typical prospect demands some kind of proof, some evidence that you can and will deliver on what you promise, that your product/service will do what you promise it will do. That doesn't mean proof positive necessarily, but it does mean convincing evidence. Here are a few of the kinds of evidence you see offered daily in advertising and TV commercials to persuade prospects to believe in the promises made:

- ✔ Guarantees.
- ✔ Free trials.
- ✔ Logical arguments.
- ✔ Technical explanations.
- ✔ Testimonials by typical users.
- ✔ Testimonials by celebrities.
- ✔ Testimonials by authority figures.
- ✔ Testimonials by government agencies and laboratories.
- ✔ Certificates and affidavits.
- ✔ Demonstrations.

> Promises must be backed by convincing evidence of some sort, evidence that the client will accept as proof that your promises are to be trusted, and as proof of your honesty and sincerity in general. That is especially essential in selling a professional service.

THIS SPECIAL CASE

We have been talking about the general case of selling and the essence of the effective sales argument in general: promise and proof. But there are kinds of promises, and not all kinds are equally effective for any given case or kind of service. The beauty consultant promises attractiveness and sex appeal, where the fashion consultant may promise a high-class image or dress that will make the client a standout. Since you are a sales consultant, it's pretty obvious that your clients want increases in their sales. But how to make a convincing promise of such a result?

Even those are general promises addressing general wants that may be presumed to exist. What you need to learn are the special problems and wants of your prospects. Remember, too, that we are not talking here about the personal, face-to-face sales presentation with an individual prospect. We are talking about making ongoing, informal presentations via those discussion groups and other electronic communications of cyberspace. In those daily exchanges of questions, answers, opinions, and information, you will learn of the needs and wants of many individuals, and you can thus gain a very special insight into what promises of benefits will be met with the greatest enthusiasm. You will be gaining valuable information that will guide you in your own contributions to the discussions. Of course, you are building your image every day via your participation. If you pay close attention, and if the members of the discussion group are true prospects for your services, you will be getting valuable guidance in positioning yourself with that group and building the image you want.

OTHER ELEMENTS

The elements that normally constitute other parts of sales presentations and appeals are principally devices for getting attention and asking for the order. Most other sales devices address one or both of these objectives. They apply to at least some extent to what you are doing in your networking, but must be adapted to network conditions.

Getting Attention

There are lots of devices for getting attention in making sales presentations via print and broadcast media, many based on what writers of fiction call "the narrative hook." That is an opening device designed to capture the reader's attention and arouse interest, or at least curiosity, at once, and so induce the reader to read on. That is why many movies and teledramas begin with some interior scene of the story that is particularly humorous, bizarre, dramatic, bloody, or otherwise startling and even strange. Writers of commercials have borrowed the idea freely and many try to work such elements into the opening of their commercials. But writers of print advertising are also admirers of the idea and use whatever textual, typographical, and graphic devices they can work into their advertising to demand the reader's attention.

These devices can be adapted to network activities, to the messages you deliver, the anecdotes you relate to others. Beware of the trap of cleverness, however. That is the trap of writing lines, slogans, aphorisms, and other copy that is clever, novel, and/or humorous, but irrelevant, or relevant only via a tortured connection or forced linkage dragged in clumsily. (One case I recall was a print advertisement that featured a photograph of a businesslike hammer and a bold line that said something about "nailing those sales.")

Sometimes, you may have some effective attention-getter that you would like to use, but have difficulty writing a headline that will provide a sensible linkage and also be a reasonable introduction to the point you want to make. In such case, you may find it most practicable to change your copy and create a natural transition. I wanted to use one of the more novel contracts I had won in the past to demonstrate that any individual can win government contracts, but the fit was not good, for the example I wanted to use did not really demonstrate that. I solved the problem by changing the orientation of the headline, making the point that the government was a customer for almost every service conceivable. I so stated in the headline and then offered the subordinate headline in bold type: THE GOVERNMENT PAID ME $6,000 TO ANSWER THEIR MAIL!" (It was a true statement and aroused immediate curiosity.)

Such an eye-opening item invariably stimulates special interest and provokes questions and discussions, opening the door to days of follow-up posts. That wins you special attention, a major objective of networking.

THE USP

USP
a distinctive feature of one's product, service, or offer.

The *USP*—originally the Unique Selling Point, but now interpreted variously as the Unique Sales Proposition, the Unique Service Program, the Unusual Service Presentation, and many other variants—can be a particularly effective attention getter. It can be novel, tinged with humor, insightful, or otherwise noteworthy, but it should be something that is attention-getting, addresses an important matter, and gives the reader a bit of food for thought. Most important, it should suggest, if not promise outright, an important benefit to the client. (It may also be or become a logo.)

> Be sure that whatever device you use to get attention and arouse interest addresses an important desire of the prospect, and not some minor advantage or benefit.

Literally, "unique" means unlike anything else in existence anywhere. For sales purpose, that strict a definition is not necessary. In a USP, unique may mean new to or outside the prospect's experience. That is, it may be unique as far as the prospect is concerned if the prospect has never before seen such a promise or claim made. For example, if you offer a 60-day free trial and no one else is offering or has offered a 60-day free trial, that is a USP. Only from you can the prospect get a 60-day free trial. One of the most famous USPs was created by young Montgomery Ward when he offered an unconditional money-back guarantee to any customer who was not satisfied. That was a startling and dramatic USP because no one had previously been bold enough to make such a promise. It had always been caveat emptor, and Ward's competitors were stunned by what they thought was a rash and foolhardy notion. When I adopted the slogan "I help you win contracts," I created a USP because no one else made an offer in such bold terms. When Joe Karbo included in his full-page advertising a copy of an affidavit by his accountant that what Karbo claimed in the advertisement about his financial journey was absolute truth, he created another soon to be widely imitated USP, one offered in a great many copycat programs, continuing to today.

What Unique Means

"Unique," as used here, can have a special meaning, other than its literal one. Many years ago, a Milwaukee brewer used the USP that in his bottling plant the bottles were all sterilized with live steam before being filled with the company's beer. When the brewer's advertising agency first proposed using this, the brewer protested that sterilizing bottles with live steam was a common practice, not a unique one. "Everybody does it," he protested to his advertising manager.

"Yes," responded the advertising man, "but nobody advertises it! That makes it unique, heretofore unknown to the reader. It is a unique practice as far as the customer knows."

> A USP must be more than merely different to be effective. It must offer some important advantage or benefit that is unique and not available elsewhere.

Of course, most USPs are imitated or at least emulated as soon as it becomes evident that they are effective and add selling power, and so the best USPs are volatile and must be replaced with new ones or modified (e.g., "The *original* 60-day free trial"). That permits you to have a permanent USP or slogan that will always distinguish you and your practice. However, nowhere is it written that you must settle for a single USP. Quite the contrary, you may have several USPs and you may create new ones regularly to fit different situations and usages. For example, if you offer ancillary products as part of your service—perhaps a newsletter, series of reports, or seminar series—you can invent a distinguishing USP for each such product. A famous USP used by the *New York Times* is the slogan "All the News That's Fit to Print." I used a USP for my proposal-writing seminars by titling them, "The *Graduate* Course in Proposal Writing." And perhaps you have passed a filling station sign that says something such as, "Last gasoline station for 45 miles." Or, if there are other stations within 45 miles, the sign may say, "Last Esso station for 45 miles."

The USP is an appropriate device to use on your business card and in all written presentations, such as brochures, letters, and proposals (especially proposals). Since each proposal is unique, offering a unique service program, it deserves to have its own unique and distinguishing USP, helping your proposal become a standout submittal. The USP may be expressed on the cover or title page of the proposal, or it may be made a running head or foot, which means it will appear at the head or foot of every page! One proposal I helped a client with carried a running foot, "The Monolithic Teleprinter." Introductory text had explained what that meant and why it delivered a substantial benefit to the client, so the running foot was a continuous reminder and reinforcement of that USP and the benefit promised.

What a USP Should Cover

A USP can cover anything of importance to a client—the guarantee, the chief benefit of what your service does for the client, an unusual payment plan, or almost anything else. Ward's USP covered the guarantee. Karbo's principal

USP (his copy included more than one) offered proof of his sincerity and the honesty of his claims, and the "live steam" USP offered assurance that the product was safe to drink.

There is no reason not to use more than one USP within a formal presentation, such as in a proposal, or even in your network discussions. Normally, your proposal includes four or more sections—an introduction, a technical discussion, the proposed program in detail, and your credentials. Each of those sections may have its own USP, stressing some reason to value what the section promises. In discussions, you can introduce the subject of USPs and even make the point that you often help clients to find or develop new USPs, especially in cases where the USP proves to be highly perishable. You might even decide that as a sales consultant you would like to become well known as "The USP Specialist." As I found the slogan "I help you win contracts" to be an effective one, you may have success with a slogan such as, "I make you stand out from your competitors" or "I write USPs that raise your image."

> You need not restrict yourself to one USP or cling to one that is aging and losing its usefulness. You may have more than one, and invent new ones as often as you wish, but don't go overboard and have so many that they distract the reader from your main point. Be sure you have a main USP, one that is distinctive and is tied closely to your overall sales strategy.

Writing a USP

Writing a USP is easy. Writing a good USP is more difficult. And writing a brilliant USP is definitely hard work, perhaps requiring a bit of creative genius or extreme good luck, but probably well worth whatever it takes to produce a brilliant USP. Of course, producing a USP is a creative process, and so there is no routine way to do so. However, some things are known about the creative process, as summarized in the following brief description.

CREATIVITY: WHAT IS IT?

Many fortunate individuals are by nature and instinct highly creative. They are individuals who do not accept the status quo as inevitable, or the latest and most accepted ways of doing things as the best ways. They are individuals who operate on a basic premise that everything can be improved, that there is always a better way waiting to be discovered or invented, and that this applies to small matters as well as to great ones. (History proves them right, of course.) In researching the nature of *creativity*, efforts have been made to interview and study the habits of highly inventive people to discover what traits they have in common that indicate or explain the inventive nature.

What such studies reveal is that invention is generally composed of three phases in the following order of occurrence:

1. Concentration.
2. Incubation.
3. Inspiration.

Concentration consists of deliberate, conscious effort to find a solution or conceive some idea. This continues as long as you are finding new ideas. I see this activity as a kind of solo brainstorming.

Incubation is suspending further conscious effort, turning the problem over to your subconscious mind to work on it.

Inspiration is the appearance in your conscious mind of a solution, that which you were seeking in the first phase.

Initially, you make an intense conscious effort to solve a problem or develop a new and better way to do

creativity
ability to solve problems and develop new ideas through concentration, incubation, and inspiration.

concentration
first step in inducing ideas by intense conscious effort to consider all ideas remotely possible.

something. Having exhausted all ideas, at least for the moment, you then dismiss the immediate problem from your mind and go about doing other things. That is the incubation phase, which leaves the problem "marinating" in your subconscious mind. At some future time, most often, it seems, when you are relaxing quietly, comes inspiration in the form of one or more new ideas that pop into your mind spontaneously.

The effect is the same as that of a common experience when trying to remember a name but being unable to do so. Later, after you have gone on to other things, and most often when you and your conscious mind are relaxing, your subconscious suddenly and unexpectedly breaks in with the name you were struggling to remember.

The lapse in time between the phases is variable and can be long or short. The theory is that your subconscious mind never forgets anything, but that it is not easy to reach and communicate with your subconscious. Hypnotists reach it by getting your conscious mind relaxed, which apparently opens the gate between the minds, and what you have just read explains much of how hypnosis works. Concentrating on the problem for a long time is another way to communicate with your subconscious and ask for help.

incubation
second step in inducing ideas and turning quest over to subconscious by dismissing subject entirely and turning to other activities, including relaxing ones.

inspiration
third step in inducing ideas by receiving sudden input from subconscious.

Creativeness can be learned and you can become more inventive and freethinking, for the mechanism is fairly well known now. But you also need the courage to swim upstream, for there are always bystanders who are eager to sneer at anything new and different.

One final observation before leaving the subject: The greatest new ideas are often the simplest ones. There are dozens of devices for binding loose sheets of documents together, for example, but no one has invented a simpler or more successful device than the lowly paper clip for temporary binding or the lowly staple for permanent binding. Inventing simple solutions is a worthy goal, and simplifications of existing functions are often the greatest advances.

> Try simplification as a path to new and better ideas. Study the existing item or process to see if it can be simplified without losing any of its useful functions.

In any case, using the three-phase creative process can be a great help in finding the most effective USPs, and is well worth the time and effort. Following is a suggested process for working on the problem and creating that brilliant USP, using the three-phase creative method described:

- ✔ Write down everything your service/offer *does* for a client. Make the list a long one.
- ✔ Scratch out everything that does not answer the question, "What does it *do*?"
- ✔ Scratch out everything that does not describe an important benefit.
- ✔ Scratch out everything that does not have an emotional element (i.e., some result the client is sure to *want*).
- ✔ Rank what is left in order of probable importance to the client, putting the greatest in importance at the top of the list.
- ✔ When you have exhausted all possibilities you can conceive, go on to other activities and allow your final list to incubate until your subconscious offers an idea or two.

The act of writing down ideas, studying them, and selecting what you think are the best ones is an excellent way to carry out the first phase—to concentrate—and then go on to the next phase.

> Try using the concentration-incubation-inspiration process to create the best USPs (and any other creative effort).

PROPOSALS IN GENERAL MARKETING

If you pursue government contracts or help clients do so, you will surely be involved in proposal writing. However, it is not only governments who solicit proposals. More and more organizations in the private sector are discovering the benefits of requesting proposals to help them select the best contractors to satisfy their needs. But even when a prospective client has not asked you for a proposal, you may volunteer to supply one, explaining that you will describe your planned program in detail, with the advantages of permitting the client to review your offer at leisure and invite his or her staff or associates to review it also.

This affords you the sales advantages described earlier, but it also is its own inducement if you are the only contender for the contract who has offered to submit a written proposal, explaining its advantages to the client. It may not occur to many clients to invite proposals, and the mere fact of offering a client the convenience of a formal written presentation often provides you an immediate sales advantage. Depending on the individual situation, you may opt to ask the prospect if he or she would welcome a written proposal, ask for permission to submit one, simply state that you will submit one, or do so without querying or announcing it. However, it is probably best to use the classic sales close of assuming approval (i.e., that the client would welcome a written proposal)—such as asking the prospect how many copies would he or she like to have, would next Tuesday be soon enough for receiving a proposal, or would a copy of the proposal on a disk be a welcome addition. That, of course, greatly reduces the probability of objections by the prospect.

> You don't have to wait to be asked for a written proposal. Treasure and appreciate the advantages of proposal writing to both yourself and your prospective client, and create you own proposal opportunities by responding to the needs of prospective clients with offers of detailed written presentations.

In this era of cyberspace communication, special proposal presentations have begun to appear. With the help of the ubiquitous desktop computer, a written presentation such as a proposal need not be produced in final form as ink on paper. Instead, there is increasing resort to "electronic ink," written presentations transmitted as e-mail, attached files, files on disks and CD-ROMs, and even as *World Wide Web* presentations made available to the client only. Thus, proposal writing and other such communications are becoming easier to create, easier to transmit, and more effective as presentations, some with color and sound. (In fact, web-like presentations are more and more frequently being sent as e-mail with the more recent e-mail software that can transmit and reproduce HTML (Hypertext Markup Language) presentations.

World Wide Web commonly accepted as part of the Internet and devoted primarily to business; casually referred to as the Web.

OTHER USES OF CYBERSPACE IN MARKETING

Of all the many ways cyberspace is used as a marketing medium today, publishing an electronic newsletter is one of the most popular and effective choices. It's relatively easy and inexpensive to create and distribute an electronic newsletter via e-mail. Most of these are distributed free of charge to any who want them, and they are used as marketing vehicles for their publishers. They are well suited to marketing consulting services, since your entire subscriber list is a prospect list that you can cultivate as a source of leads. And, of course, if you build a large enough circulation, you have created an adequately sized network of your own, as well as a means for creating and building your professional image as a capable and available consultant. For a distribution list of a few dozen, you can do the distribution yourself via e-mail. (Most e-mail systems can handle bulk transmissions of a few dozen.) If the circulation list grows into hundreds of names and larger—even into many thousands—there are services available to handle the distribution for you through special equipment.

> The easiest, least costly promotional medium to use in cyberspace is probably the electronic newsletter. If your circulation list is small, you can handle the whole thing from your desk. If it grows larger, you can get a distribution service at reasonable rates.

WEB SITES

The most common business use of cyberspace (after e-mail) is for web sites (although many individuals have web sites as a kind of personal hobby). Hardly any business of size does not have a web site, and a great many very small businesses also have their own web sites. Web sites now number in hundreds of millions.

In one respect, a web site resembles a billboard along the highway. Most open with a colorful display. However, a sophisticated web site is more than an announcement: It is a two-way communication device, too, since you can click items on it to learn more, fill out forms, and talk back in that manner. Moreover, it can include sound.

Costs are relatively modest. You normally need a host—someone to store the information in a host computer available to anyone with the right URL (Uniform Resource Locator or web address). That can cost you as little as $10 per month for a small site of a few frames. You can develop your own site or you can hire any of the many services available to create a site for you.

There is nothing magical about a web site. Once created, it does nothing on its own. Rarely do people just happen across it; they have to deliberately seek it out. (The Internet is not a superhighway at all; it is a jumble of back roads in almost random display.) That means that for a significant number of people to seek out your site so that it represents effective sales promotion, you have to advertise it in some manner. You will find numerous examples of how others advertise their sites. Many include their site address in their signature, a brief message attached automatically to each of their e-mails. Others run classified advertisements reporting the kinds of information available at their sites. Many trade references with other site owners.

> A web site of your own is easy enough to create and maintain, and it can be an effective marketing tool, but it requires sustained effort and expense to attract enough visitors to make it work for you. Be prepared to supply that effort and expense before you undertake to create a web site of your own.

newsgroups
many thousands of electronic communications and discussion groups, using e-mail and resembling electronic bulletin boards of pre-Internet days.

NEWSGROUPS

Still another kind of discussion group is the *newsgroup*. There are many thousands of these, as there are of other kinds of groups. A great many are on frivolous subjects and a great many are inactive, never having captured many participants. But there are also a great many that are quite serious and are quite active, with many dedicated correspondents. These may be most useful to you in your networking, building your image and visibility. As in the case of e-mail, there is an abundance of software programs available to search through and select newsgroups. Usually your ISP (Internet service provider) will have furnished you software for e-mail and newsgroups, although they will normally be available via your browser.

Chapter

7

Finding Your Niches

Most fields today are far too large and diverse for an independent consultant to attempt to serve. Rather, you must select and pursue specific market segments or niches that are especially right for you.

MARKETS AND NICHES

Two major problems face the new independent consultant contemplating a practice in almost any field today: choosing markets to pursue and choosing service specialties to offer to prospective clients. In most cases, these two areas are so closely related to each other that they are aspects of the same problem. However, it makes sense to address the marketing aspect—winning clients—as the more immediate need, as it is in all business ventures in general.

Markets are all but unlimited geographically in these days of travel and communication that have made the whole world a village. Only the largest consulting organizations can even attempt to cover entire markets, with all their specialties and assortment of needs. But in the sales field, this is an even more challenging consideration, for marketing is something every organization must do (i.e., almost everyone is a potential client). Even nonprofit organizations run marketing campaigns in quest of donors, new members, votes, and other items that are, for them, what sales are for profit-making organizations. Their survival also depends on their success in marketing to win the members, votes, volunteers, donations, or whatever it is that is their equivalent of the sales that for-profit organizations pursue.

Markets are made up of many kinds of customers with many different kinds of needs, problems, and wants. The mail order seller needs different kinds of support than does the hardware chain or the appliance retailer. Each group with a common need—for example, retailers of big-tag items or new businesses trying to develop a standard sales posture—becomes a distinctive market segment, a niche in the market. In doing business with the government, for example, I found many government offices and agencies were good markets for custom training material, and so I became especially watchful for those sales opportunities. Agencies that needed and bought the writing of custom training materials became a major niche market for me, one in which I could prosper. For a long time, that niche provided the bulk of my custom writing contracts.

As an independent practitioner, you will have to discover those market niches that are most hospitable to you as a contractor. They can be and should be a major consideration in planning your independent sales consulting practice. You will need to identify one or more—as many as you need to represent a sufficiently large market to keep you busy supplying your services. That does not preclude your making changes, as you gain experience and perhaps find that the niches you chose are not the best ones for your purposes or that there have been significant changes in your market. On the contrary, it is quite likely that your first few tentative choices of market niches will be less productive than some you will later discover, so no matter how good your first choices appear to be, you should always reevaluate your earlier choices and be ready to make changes or to take advantage of new and better niches that you discover. You can't be sure that you have captured or chosen the best niches of those available until you have examined and tested them all. Assume that the best is yet to come, and keep looking until you think you have examined all and chosen the best.

> Niche markets are usually special in both size and needs—that is, they are relatively small segments of the market needing something special in what they require. That is what makes the niche a special one.

ANOTHER KIND OF NICHE

Market niches are only one of two kinds of niches you must identify. *Service niches* are the other. In sales consulting, as in most fields today, a great variety of services are needed and offered as consulting specialties: *Copywriting*, training sales staffs, designing and managing campaigns, organizing and managing trade show promotions, building direct mail productions, and creating sales literature are just a few of the services for which there is a demand. In sales consulting, as in most fields, it is all but impossible for you to be a provider of all the conceivable services, so you must decide what services you wish to offer your prospective clients. When agencies that bought the writing of training materials became a major market niche for me, doing that kind of writing for clients became a service niche for me.

Usually the market niche will dictate the service niche in this manner. However, be careful in identifying your service niches to be sure that they are completely compatible with your chosen market niches. (It is possible that your market niche may prove to offer opportunities to identify more than one service niche.) If your field is direct mail, for example, you have to be sure that you have chosen market niches that include a population of those who are in direct mail or want to get into that field.

Incidentally, that suggests a special market niche: There are direct mail consultants who specialize in help-

service niche
a segment of all the services possible selected as one's specialty.

copywriting
writing advertising and promotional copy, or sell copy.

ing people break into the direct mail field or add direct mail to the marketing programs they already use. That is true in all fields. There is always a market for services to help aspirants break into a field that is new to them, just as I found many clients who wanted my help in learning how to write proposals. If you make it a service to help clients break into a field that is new to them, that will mean you will be, in effect, offering training as a service to clients. Be prepared to take advantage of that probability.

The two niches, markets and services, are thus not only related to each other, but are often all but identical, aspects of the same thing: Direct mail, for example, identifies both the market segment and the set of services.

> You will need to identify both the market niches and the service niches you will address as a sales consultant. They must, of course, be compatible with each other.

WHICH NICHE COMES FIRST?

If you have decided in advance what services you will offer, you will be looking for the market niches that match those services. If, for example, you have a good track record in warehouse sales, you will want to look for the kinds of organizations likely to be interested in that—department stores, home furnishings sellers, and furniture retailers, for example. But just what do you do to support warehouse sales? Organize them? Advertise and promote them to create the traffic? Conduct them? Are you an auctioneer? Do you train staff people in conducting a warehouse sale? Lecture to trade associations on the subject? All of these?

On the other hand, you might go at this the other way, choosing the market segments first and then deciding what services you can and should offer. If you are experienced at helping large organizations conduct big sales programs, you know what the general nature of your niche market is, but you need to decide just what kinds of organizations you want to pursue and to what services they are likely to be most receptive.

You may have to assemble two or more skills and abilities you have to define the services you want to offer. You may, for example, be experienced as a trainer and have heavy background in selling services to business firms. You will then want to seek market niches of business organizations that sell services to other businesses. They will be your initial targets. In time, you may discover that pursuing one type of such organization works better for you than pursuing other types, as I discovered that computer programming companies were more receptive to what I had to offer than electronics companies were.

NONPROFITS ALSO HAVE SALES NEEDS

Usually we associate sales with profit-making organizations pursuing orders from customers. However, nonprofit organizations—unions, trade groups, associations, government agencies, quasi-government agencies, and others—must have marketing programs of their own to recruit members, win pledges from donors, solicit votes, and otherwise pursue the equivalent of sales (although they are not referred to as sales, but are memberships, votes, donations, etc.). In fact, nonprofit organizations are often excellent prospects for your services. They need to market, just as for-profit organizations do, and quite often you will find that they are truly inexperienced in marketing and need a great deal of help. Be alert for opportunities in that field.

The client considering the use of consulting help normally looks for and hopes to find a consultant whose specialty coincides closely with the client's field. The closer your specialty matches the client's idea of what he or she needs, the more attractive you are to the client as the right consultant. It may be true, too, that organizations to whom the thought of using consultants is a new idea may be intrigued enough to want to try it, and may find your experience as a sales expert especially interesting and attractive if it is in a closely relevant field or kind of sales experience.

> Nonprofit organizations also need to market, and they are often the best prospects for your services as a sales consultant to help them attract new members, win donations, attract voters, and otherwise do the marketing nonprofits must do.

MAKE YOUR SPECIALTY CLEAR

So your consulting specialty is often itself a major element in your professional image and your appeal. Consequently, the ability to identify your specialty clearly is a major consideration influencing a client in choosing a consultant. For example, Elmer Wheeler, "America's greatest salesman," was addressing retail sales and obviously had the consumer in mind when he coined such often-quoted slogans as "Sell the sizzle, not the steak," and he also confirmed that same impression when he helped a merchant sell off an oversupply of long underwear by advertising, "They don't itch." Wheeler had a talent for finding the short, hard-hitting sales message that got to the heart of the matter with the benefit promised, with consumer motivation. Those who sought his help understood that talent of his quite clearly. Wheeler's market was those organizations that sold whatever they sold to the public at large, since his slogans and hot buttons were always aimed to define the most effective emotional appeals to the consumer, as the two examples used here demonstrate.

IDENTIFY INTENDED CLIENTS

There are other considerations in selecting your specialty and market. Your specialty may itself identify those who are most likely to be good prospects as clients for your special skills and services. Still, prospective clients you had never considered will often come up with projects and services that had not occurred to you. A prospect who has sold primarily through dealers and representatives or commission salespeople of one sort or another may suddenly become interested in trying a direct response sales effort, and ask if you can help organize such a program. You will then have to decide whether to venture into this new arena, if you have never worked in direct response marketing. You need to consider how broad a market you can cover effectively and in which areas you are most experienced, most knowledgeable, and most confident. Ask yourself, also, in which market segments you see the best potential—greatest number of prospective clients and easiest accessibility. Even a niche market and niche service must be large enough to be worth making a specialty of it. Also, do not overlook the great business potential of those prospective clients with whom you are personally acquainted. You have probably built a large list of business acquaintances over the years, so the years of selling to many people in many companies can be a "who to" asset, as well as a how-to one.)

USE WORKSHEETS FOR ANALYSIS

These are all factors you must consider and questions to ask yourself. One way to analyze this objectively is by writing it out on worksheets. When you see the data arrayed, it is easier to set your own biases and premises aside and study the alternatives. Figure 7.1 is a sample worksheet you might use or modify to fit your own situation. The first item, for example, refers to the general level at which you have the greatest experience, skills,

FIGURE 7.1   Worksheet for self-analysis.

Estimated Strengths as a Sales Consultant
(Rank from 1 to 10, with 10 the greatest strength)

General Level/Category of Sales Activities
Retail: _____   Wholesale: _____   Both: _____   Nonprofit: _____
Direct Response, Mail: _____   Direct Response, Internet: _____
Other Direct Response: _____
Special Promotions: _____ International Sales: _____ Online Sales: ____

Other:_____
_____
_____

Types of Items
Consumer products: ____ Consumer services: ___ Both: _____
Other products: _____   Other services: _____   Intangibles: _____
Hard goods: _____   Soft goods: _____   Both: _____
Small-tag sales: _____   Big-tag sales: _____   Both: _____

Other: _____
_____
_____

Types of Sales and Services
Strategies: _____   Program design: _____   Advertising: _____
Training: _____   Research: _____   Web design: _____

Other: _____
_____
_____

Existing Contacts
Industries/organizations where I know a great many executives and
buyers and/or am myself well known to many executives and buyers:
_____
_____
_____
_____
_____
_____

past successes, and other such concerns. "Special promotions" refers to any of the possible situations outside the normal channels of distribution, such as special sales to close out surplus goods (e.g., warehouse sales, auctions, and contests). Each of these is a category, at least in the typical client's view, that calls for certain special experience and knowledge.

YOU MAY HAVE MORE THAN ONE CLASS OF CLIENTS

Notice that "both" is a choice in some categories. You may have such extensive sales experience that "both" is a viable choice. Ordinarily, you do better as a consultant by focusing rather sharply and avoiding any hint of being a generalist who can do it all, so you should think hard about being "both" in any of these categories. (There are ways to broaden your field without appearing to be a jack-of-all-trades consultant, but for now let's stick with basic principles.)

Having chosen the general categories in which you believe yourself to have the greatest strengths, you must choose the services that you will feature in your offer to help clients. Here, you will have to seek a balance to avoid making your chosen share of the market appear to be too broad or too narrow. Notice the word "appear" here. The heart of the matter is not whether you are truly broad in your capabilities, but rather your appearance, as the client perceives you. You need to focus sharply on a specialty or two. Too broad a stated main target means that you will appear to prospects as a sales generalist, which reduces your image and appeal as the specialist a consultant is presumed to be. Too narrow a market share means too small a market for your services. You must strike a reasonable balance between the extremes, and to do so, you may have to make a tentative selection and modify it as experience dictates. The usual tendency is to address too wide a market, but that is not a bad thing if you do so consciously, aware that you will probably narrow your market as experience points you to the targets that give you the best results.

Be aware that most clients will tend to see you as a one-service specialist, even when you try to make it clear that you have several services to offer. In one case, a client called on us a number of times to quote writing tasks in support of its publications department, most of which we were retained to provide. However, I learned that this client often invited quotations for artwork for his publications, but never invited us to bid for these. I called on the head of that department one day to ask why we were not invited to bid for a service that we had made clear was one of the general array of publications services we provided. The gentleman told me that it had not occurred to him that we might be a source for art support. This despite the fact that he had once worked for me and knew our organization!

> In all matters, but especially in marketing, you must always be conscious of the prospect's perception of what you offer. You will often be surprised at how the prospect categorizes you and what you do.

BE PREPARED TO MODIFY FIRST CHOICES

You usually can't be sure of where and what the best choices are until you make a beginning, so don't be too confident that you know in advance your best markets and services. Your natural tendency will be to address those markets in which you have had the most experience. I did so when I began to market my services as a writer-consultant, choosing to target high-tech companies because that is where my prior experience pointed me as a former employee of a number of such companies. I soon found, however, that government agencies, small and large, were a better market for me, especially in buying training materials. I began to change my marketing focus as a result, doing a great deal more business with the government. Along the same lines, it was a query from a manager in a major electronics manufacturing firm that made me aware of a potential market for custom seminars in proposal writing. As it happened, I failed completely to close this first lead for a custom proposal-writing seminar or several similar leads that followed. Soon enough, it made me realize that I must be doing something quite wrong that caused me to strike out each time. I see failures as the lessons that constitute education, and these failures compelled me to educate myself by doing some serious thinking and experimenting until I found a way to enter this market successfully.

CONSIDER THE CLIENT'S INTERESTS

Originally, invited to quote a figure for delivering an in-house seminar on proposal writing, I had asked for what I thought to be a modest compensation that included a small sum for customizing my standard proposal-writing seminar to the client's needs. My quotation was rejected by the executive who had originally made the inquiry. After having the same experience with others who had shown similar interest in having my seminar delivered to their staffs in-house, I soon realized that the problem was this: Few prospects were going to pay me to create a custom seminar for them that they would probably use only once. It was not the price, for that was modest enough, but the principle to which they objected. I therefore rethought the whole proposition and developed an entirely different approach, one that would not make a charge for custom development. Instead, I named a flat figure, plus expenses, for delivering my standard full-day seminar, which I would customize for them without charge, and I offered the client the following features and inducements:

- ✔ If the client would send me a set of brochures and other literature, I would familiarize myself in advance with the client's normal operations and needs.
- ✔ On the basis of that familiarization, I would customize my presentation spontaneously by selecting examples appropriate to the client's own operations and needs.
- ✔ I would provide the client with one loose-leaf master copy of my copyright 60-page seminar manual/workbook with permission to duplicate it in enough copies to present one to each attendee of the presentation.
- ✔ All of this would be provided for one flat fee covering my full day on the platform plus whatever expenses I would incur for travel, food, and lodging.

That approach worked quite well. I asked for enough of a fee to compensate myself for any time I had to invest in reading the client's literature and familiarizing myself with the company and its activities. (The acceptance of this approach confirmed that the cost was not the sticking point.) I never lost another bid to present a seminar to a group as a consulting service, using this approach. If you know your subject well enough to customize it spontaneously while on the platform delivering it, you should have no problem with this.

The early period in your new venture is a valuable learning experience, if you accept that you will almost surely make mistakes or at least that you do not have all the answers yet, but you take advantage of the experiences and use them as lessons in what to do and what not to do.

CLOSING

It is not my intention to teach the art of selling here, for it is a premise of this book that the reader is a sales professional. However, it seems appropriate to point out something I learned about closing in connection with the foregoing tale. At the time the flat fee I asked for was $1,000, which made a few individuals gasp a bit, for that was a high daily rate for an independent consultant in those days. However, in keeping with good sales tactics, I carefully avoided mentioning the cost, waiting for the prospect to ask, and even then managed to avoid stating my fee until I was ready to do so (i.e., had prepared the client). Then, I first reminded the client of everything he or she was to get for that price, enumerating each item and stating all that was for "only" $1,000 for everything and a complete day of my time, with no charge for travel time. I also mentioned at that time some special tips I would impart to the attendees, including a way to appear to be the low bidder although you may not be, and a few tips on how to avoid contract disputes and accelerate payment of your invoices. That made the fee appear to be not at all outrageous. (I had, over the years, noted a few things of which even experienced government marketers and proposal writers appeared to be unaware, and I featured these in my seminars.)

SOME CRITERIA FOR IDENTIFYING A NICHE MARKET

The worksheet should have given you a better idea of some of the many ways in which a market segment may be distinguished as a promising niche to address. A niche is any segment of the market that has some distinguishing characteristic, usually a need, that is different enough to require special attention and effort to capture a worthwhile share of its sales potential. A market segment is a niche only in comparison with other measures, such as the size of the consulting organization. That does not mean that the niche must be made up of small companies. A niche market may be a need that a few large companies (and only a relative few) have. I found, for example, that it was not only small companies that were markets for my proposal writing seminars; even a few large companies were markets for training seminars in proposal writing. Those companies were part of my niche market, and the successful sales approach I had developed for the small companies worked equally well with the large ones.

I soon found a niche within that niche in the multi-office company that wanted me to make my seminar presentation to several of their branch offices, after I had delivered it to the home office and top executives had sat in on it. I also discovered certain key points that made a great impression on the higher-level executives, and so I made sure that those points were prominent and noted. (One executive remarked to me that one key point I stressed, one of the special tips that I promised to reveal, was worth the time and cost of the entire day.) That led to multiple presentations for the same client, in some cases. Even if a company did not have a web of small offices, it had many departments and sometimes retained me to present my seminar to each department.

You may select as a niche those companies of a certain maximum size in a certain sales specialty, such as small businesses in direct mail, to whom you offer general services. The distinguishing feature, in that case, is that they are small direct-mail sales organizations. (In some cases, the small companies are more receptive to offers of help than are their large competitors.) Or they may be companies of any size that use premium campaigns and invite services to help them develop new ideas. That feature, premium campaigns, is the distinguishing one in the latter case.

The best niche is often a market segment neglected by your large competitors as too small in which to invest marketing expense and effort, but that measure is not true for your efforts as an independent consultant. That segment may be a comfortable size for your efforts and marketing capability.

In general, a niche is generally a small segment of the market overall, and it may well be a niche because it is too small to be profitable for your large competitors to pursue. A major advertising agency, for example, does not normally pursue small accounts because the income of the major advertising agencies is based on their clients' purchases of large amounts of advertising space or time, which a small business normally does not buy in large quantity. So a large advertising agency seeks to acquire only those clients that buy large quantities of media time and space. Small agencies tend to the needs of the smaller companies on a different basis—time and material charges for their services.

Although too small to interest a large consulting company, a niche may be large enough to be the main market for smaller organizations or independent consultants such as yourself. The home-based small business, for example, might well be an important niche market for you as an independent sales consultant.

It is possible that serving clients in a single niche market would alone support your practice, or you may find it better to pursue and service several niche markets. In fact, you may find it highly advisable to target several niches so as to avoid the hazard of having all your eggs in one basket. That can be as great a hazard to your ultimate success as having a single major client monopolizing your time, so that the loss of that client, for whatever reason, would be a disaster for you. Your security is better preserved by gaining the independence of having many clients or diverse enough services so that loss of any single client does not hurt you seriously.

The Quest for Niches

There is no sure way of finding the best niches other than being thoroughly familiar with the market spectrum, doing a detailed market analysis, or simply learning the market through long experience. Even then you might easily overlook or fail to detect a niche that might be a useful one for you. However, often the discovery of a promising niche is simply serendipity, the fortunate accidental discovery of something you were not knowingly pursuing but were alert enough to recognize quickly. Thus, serendipity is not necessarily completely random or uncontrolled; it is possible to introduce at least some small measure of influence to increase its occurrence. Like fortune, opportunity of all sorts favors the prepared mind—is dependent on it, in fact—so that you recognize niches when you happen across them. You can train your subconscious to be alert for such random discoveries. Prepare your subconscious for this by remembering to be always alert for such opportunities, seeking them. Do this consciously and continuously, with focus and concentration, for a time, and you will find that your mind becomes almost instinctively alert for market opportunities without further conscious effort.

Evaluating Niches

The most general characteristic of a market niche is size relative to the whole market, but there is more to it than size alone. There is also the distinguishing characteristic(s) of whatever measures you must take to pursue it as a special market. There may be some special measure necessary to reach the prospects in the niche and make your offer to them, some special service that the rest of the market does not ask for or require, or some other special thing you must do to make sales in that niche. It is the fact of the need to do something in particular to sell to it that makes it a niche. It is because those measures are needed to pursue the market represented by that niche that your competitors choose not to pursue it, even if they are aware of its existence. So you must evaluate the niche for yourself to decide whether you will pursue it. You may find that the niche is far less desirable a target than you thought, or you may find the opposite—that the niche has some particular benefit to offer you. Basic questions to ask yourself in evaluating the niche as a possible market target might include these:

- ✔ What special sales problems do companies in the niche have? What sales problems must I solve for clients there?
- ✔ Is the niche large enough in probable sales volume to be worth the effort to pursue it?
- ✔ What are the possible/probable other benefits (than sales per se) of winning sales in it? Would it open the door to other opportunities for me, such as provide me with a new capability I could probably sell to the broader market?
- ✔ How much time and expense will it take to make the effort? What is my probable exposure (risk)?
- ✔ What does the competition in the niche appear to be? With whom would I have to compete?
- ✔ Do I have any advantages (over others) in winning some significant part of the niche's business?

These are most basic questions, and are by no means the only ones you might ask yourself before committing time and other resources to pursuit of a given niche market, especially if you are unable to get very much information to answer the questions. Answers to these questions should guide you in making sensible decisions about choosing market targets, especially in the case of evaluating niches.

EMULATE OR INNOVATE?

Oil baron John D. Rockefeller Sr. was reported to have advocated, as a formula for success, that one observe what someone else is doing successfully and then set about to do that same thing but do it far better than the other party is doing it. Undoubtedly, emulation is one way to success, and we can see it at work every day. But then there is an alternate formula of innovation or offering something new and different than your competitors offer. That, too, we see almost daily as a road to success. Sometimes that successful new idea is born almost by accident, as someone stumbles onto it or is pushed into it by fate. But it can be and often is a deliberate development, as someone perceives a want that is not being satisfied and devises a way to satisfy it, perhaps even creating a new market niche in so doing.

Somers White, a well-known speaker and consultant with a career background in banking, recently wrote in the public speakers' trade periodical *Sharing Ideas* (published by Royal Publishing, P.O. Box 398, Glendora, CA 91740) an article on niche marketing. He related how he created a niche market of his own by developing what he called a *niche program* that he titled "Negotiating for Money." (He reported that it was often called "How to Deal More Effectively with Bankers and Lenders" or "How to Have Bankers and Lenders Begging to Give You Money.") With such descriptions, small wonder that his niche program was a great success. Who would not want to sit in on such a program and learn how to persuade bankers to approve loan applications?

The idea of developing niche programs of your own is an exciting one, and it should stir your imagination. Think of it as creating new service niches, along the philosophical lines of the frequent admonition to "find a need and fill it," rather than copying what someone else is already doing. (Exception: Sometimes finding a way to do it better is actually the creation of something new, and is innovation, rather than emulation.) Obviously, you will have no competition, at least not immediately. Too, as a new and unique idea it offers an excellent possibility to create a powerful USP (see Chapter 6).

niche program
program or special service that attracts so many participants that it becomes a market niche of its own, a private niche.

You need not necessarily wait to discover niche markets. You can create your own niche markets by developing your own niche programs to fill needs.

A Set of Niches

Rita Risser, whose specialty is legal training for managers, sees her own niche markets as falling into three categories: a topic niche or specialty that enables her to achieve status as an expert in the topic; a market niche, in which she applies her special abilities to a selected industry (high tech, in her case); and a geographical niche, which, in her case, means pursuing clients in her own region because she prefers not to travel.

> You can define or classify niches in various ways, and it may help you get a firmer fix on your market by defining a set of niches as your market(s).

Getting Ideas for Niche Programs

You can work at getting ideas for new niche programs in the same way that you pursue the conceiving of new ideas for any activity (see Chapter 6). However, ideas for niche programs may grow out of the ancillary services you develop (see Chapter 9). In developing ancillary services, you will be presenting and discussing ideas in a newsletter, from the lecture platform, via e-mail, or through any other ancillary activity. When you find your audience especially interested in and responding enthusiastically to some new idea, you may have the germ of an original and unique niche program and thereby the opening of a new and exclusive niche market. But ideas for such programs may come at any time from any source, even serendipitously.

> Put the creative stimuli of concentration, incubation, and inspiration (see Chapter 6) to work in helping you get ideas for new and powerful niche programs.

The idea for a proposal writing seminar came to me unexpectedly. It ultimately proved to be a niche program and opened a new niche market for me. It came about in this way:

I had been asked to be one of several guest speakers at a seminar on marketing to the government. Although I needed to give only an hour to the program, I was well experienced in the subject and interested enough to want to hear what the other speakers had to say on the subject, and so I decided to attend the entire seminar.

I was shocked to hear some of the most often repeated but also most outrageously ridiculous myths propagated by speakers who preceded me. In substance, while they did not say that government contracts were "fixed," they suggested strongly that it was futile to enter into a contest for a government contract if one had not been schmoozing the agency's key people and reached an "understanding" in advance, even to having been "in on" the procurement long before it was announced. (My experience was very much to the contrary, since I had won many contracts with proposals I had written as a complete dark horse competitor, totally unknown to the client before submitting my proposal.) Then, having assured the audience that the proposal is little more than a formality and had little to do with the award, they set forth to give the audience some tips on how to write winning proposals! They obviously did not see this paradox in their presentations.

I was thus forced to be extremely tactful in my own presentation to avoid open controversy on the platform (direct contradiction of what earlier speakers had said) and yet offer what I believed to be the truth about proposal writing, which was almost directly opposite to what my predecessors on that platform had been telling the audience that morning.

Creating My Own Niche Market

It was that experience, especially the frustration of tap dancing my way around a direct refutation of what the audience had been listening to so far that morning, that caused me to decide that I would have to stage my own seminar to do what I had wanted so badly to do that day: to tell the truth, as my own successful experience had long ago revealed it to me, about government contracting and proposal writing. I therefore did so organize my first such seminar not long after that morning's experience, and it was successful enough to bear repeating and to become perpetuated as a major service I provided for several years after. I had thus created a successful niche service/ niche program/niche market, although I never thought of it in those terms until I read Somers White's article and his creative coinage.

Chapter

Selling to the Government and Proposal Writing

The government does business with the largest corporations in the world, but it also spends billions with small companies and even with contracts to individuals. It is a market for anyone and everyone.

WHAT IS "THE GOVERNMENT"?

Reference to "the government" is generally taken to mean the U.S. government, our federal governing bureaucracy. It is a great institution, representing the world's single superpower, the government of the wealthiest nation in the world, and the largest customer in the world, spending well over $200 billion annually to buy goods and services from organizations in the private sector.

However, that is only one of our many governments. There are something on the order of 86,000 governments in the United States, according to Census Bureau reports, which include all state and local governments—counties, cities, towns, townships, districts, and special districts—all of which do most of their own buying. The government market is thus a truly huge one in numbers, as well as in dollars.

THE WORLD'S BIGGEST MARKET

Even without regard to all the other entities listed here as elements of the government market, the U.S. federal government alone is the largest customer in the world—the largest in both total dollars spent and variety of goods and services. The federal procurement budget has already been identified as well in excess of $200 billion per year, but even that is not all of it for there are several off-budget activities that are not counted in that figure: There is the Postal Service, which is a separate government corporation and spends many more billions, and there are a few other government agencies whose procurements are on separate budgets of their own. The state and local governments represent probably more than twice as much as the federal government in purchasing goods and services in the marketplace. So the total government spending is well in excess of $650 billion annually, and that increases steadily as our population continues to grow.

> The government represents many markets, so voluminous and diverse that almost anyone in business, smallest or largest, can find contract opportunities. Many entrepreneurs do all their business with government agencies.

None of these thousands of government entities is a commercial or for-profit business, although the Postal Service, as a government corporation, tries to take in enough money to cover all its expenses and be self-supporting. (The Postal Service and the Federal Supply Service actually have marketing departments.) The military services often spend large sums of money in commercial advertising and other such sales activities to support their recruiting, which is itself a marketing function, meant to attract recruits as their version of "sales."

That government agencies and programs are nonprofit organizations and activities doesn't change the fact that they do market in a very real sense, and whereas the major markets for sales consultants are the commercial organizations operated for profit, the nonprofit organizations that market to attract recruits, members, volunteers, votes, and donations to carry out their missions often need sales support, too. Thus many other organizations—associations, labor unions, government agencies, charities, and other nonprofit entities—are viable markets for independent sales consultants and their services.

It may seem that there would be only limited opportunity for a sales consultant to find and win government contracts. However, there is more here than meets the eye of the individual not yet familiar with government procurement. In fact, government agencies contract with consultants of many kinds for a variety of duties. There are literally thousands of government agencies, and the services they buy are so varied that there are frequent opportunities you would never expect. For example, on one occasion, I was retained by a government agency to answer its mail, and another agency hired a contractor to answer both its telephones and its mail. Some agencies hire consultants to help them write their *requests for proposals* (RFPs), and some hire consultants to help review and evaluate the proposals they receive. Closely allied to sales promotions are publicity campaigns carried out by all sorts of organizations, and as a sales consultant your abilities will often qualify you to pursue contracts for a role in this kind of activity, too.

 **request for proposal (RFP)** an invitation to compete for a contract to satisfy a stated requirement of the requester.

It is all but impossible to anticipate all the needs government agencies encounter and for which they contract with organizations and individuals in the private sector. One government agency contracted to rent mules and handlers. Another contracted with a theatrical troupe to present a typical eighteenth-century family in a National Park Service memorial house. And on at least one occasion, a military unit contracted with a theatrical agency in the private sector to provide go-go dancers for a servicemen's club. And so one cannot reliably predict what services government agencies will and will not buy, or how you might apply your talents to help government agencies satisfy their needs.

I started out to pursue general writing opportunities in government agencies, and soon found that there was a great demand for the development of training materials, and relatively few skilled writers were pursuing opportunities there. And so although I claimed no special expertise as a teacher or trainer, I learned to adapt my writing abilities to the design and development of how-to manuals, lecture guides, programmed instruction, and other training tools and instruments.

Certainly, an enterprising sales consultant who makes the marketing effort will find government needs he or she might pursue as a sales opportunity. In addition to sales services to support military recruiting needs, you will find, if you research the market thoroughly, many other requirements for which your sales experience qualifies you, such as writing brochures and pamphlets and training people in sales functions.

Still, even that represents the smaller portion of the opportunities to put your sales skills to work in connection with government procurement. That will become clearer as we explore how government agencies buy services and products, and as we identify business opportunities therein for independent sales consultants. Many government needs are unpredictable, so there is no good alternative to continuous market research, if you are to learn of all opportunities.

Serendipity—unexpected and fortuitous opportunity—is a common factor in winning government-connected business windfalls. Alert and continuous market research—monitoring the government markets—is necessary to help good fortune find you.

There is another side to this prospect of government contracts, but we'll come to that after we explore what and how government agencies normally buy. What is described here reflects the needs and purchasing practices of the federal government agencies, but the state and local governments follow pretty much the same lines as the federal agencies do in procurement. There may be certain differences, principally this one: The federal government has its procurement thoroughly decentralized so that most government agencies have their own procurement offices and do their own buying. Other governments, at state and local levels, tend to buy centrally through their own supply departments, although there are exceptions to this.

WHAT THE GOVERNMENT BUYS

Government needs are organized into supply groups for products of various kinds, and into categories of services where it is a service that is the primary objective of a procurement. Here, for example, are the kinds of needs and contract categories normally listed in the *Commerce Business Daily* or *CBD*, a Department of Commerce publication in which the government lists its needs and opportunities for the procurement of services every day:

A—Research and Development.

B—Special Studies and Analyses—Not R&D.

C—Architect and Engineering Services— Construction.

D—Automatic Data Processing and Telecommunication Services.

F—Natural Resources and Conservation Services.

H—Quality Control, Testing, and Inspection Services.

J—Maintenance, Repair, and Rebuilding of Equipment.

K—Modification of Equipment.

L—Technical Representative Services.

M—Operation of Government-Owned Facilities.

Q—Medical Services.

R—Professional, Administrative, and Management Support Services.

S—Utilities and Housekeeping Services.

T—Photographic, Mapping, Printing, and Publication Services.

U—Education and Training Services.

V—Transportation, Travel, and Relocation Services.

W—Lease or Rental of Equipment.

X—Lease or Rental of Facilities.

Y—Construction of Structures and Facilities.

Z—Maintenance, Repair, or Alteration of Real Property.

For products, there is a list of supply groups, numbering approximately 100 categories of supply. Following is just a partial list:

13—Ammunition and Explosives.

15—Aircraft and Airframe Structural Components.

16—Aircraft Components and Accessories.

17—Aircraft Launching, Landing, and Ground Handling Equipment.

19—Ships, Small Craft, Pontoons, and Floating Docks.

20—Ships and Marine Equipment.

25—Vehicular Equipment Components.

28—Engines, Turbines, and Components.

29—Engine Accessories.

30—Mechanical Power Transmission Equipment.

31—Bearings.

34—Metalworking Machinery.

36—Special Industry Machinery.

38—Construction, Mining, Excavating, and Highway Maintenance Equipment.

39—Materials Handling Equipment.

40—Rope, Cable, Chain, and Fittings.

41—Refrigeration, Air-Conditioning, and Air-Circulating Equipment.

43—Pumps and Compressors.

44—Furnace, Steam Plant, Drying Equipment, and Nuclear Reactors.

47—Pipe, Tubing, Hose, and Fittings.

The government market—markets, really, for there are many different ones represented—is so diverse that almost anyone in business, from the smallest to the largest enterprise, can find at least occasional contract opportunities, and many entrepreneurs do all their business with government agencies.

HOW THE GOVERNMENT BUYS

The goods and services procured by government agencies are purchased in several ways. Standard items—commodities—for which detailed specifications exist or can be stated by the agency are generally bought by sealed bids, opened publicly, with the low bidder normally awarded the contract. Items for which there are no existing detailed specifications and the agency cannot provide such specifications must be custom designed, and so are generally bought by negotiation using the following general process (although details may vary from one agency to another, and there are exceptions of various kinds under different sets of circumstances):

1. The agency issues an RFP (request for proposal), describing the need as accurately as possible and asking contenders for the contract to offer their analysis of what the agency needs and how they, the contractors, propose to go about satisfying the need. (This usually requires that the contractor write a proposal that presents a detailed program and details of estimated costs.)

2. The agency reviews the proposals and rates them. It rates them technically first, but also considers the cost of the program and factors that into the final judgment of overall quality of the proposal. Evaluation systems vary, but in most cases the estimated technical quality of the proposed program—viability of the proposed program, quality of proposer's credentials, and related factors— merits a higher priority than cost does, as long as the cost is in the "competitive range" (or ballpark) with reference to the agency's budget for the program. (That represents the agency's estimate of what the program should cost.)

3. The agency then conducts negotiations with one or more of those whose proposals are considered acceptable, often beginning with an invitation to each contender to submit his or her best and final offer. (That BAFO, however, is often not mentioned when inviting a proposer in to discuss his or her proposal, but is requested only after that discussion, as the meeting is about to end.)

This process may culminate in a choice of a single contractor for final negotiations, or negotiations may be conducted with more than one proposer, although only one contract will result. Keep in mind that despite the voluminous set of Federal Acquisition Regulations (FAR), practices and policies vary widely from one agency to another.

The art of winning contracts via a proposal competition is the art of proposal writing and related functions of marketing and negotiating. While we may refer to the process as "proposal writing," writing skill per se is a

> Government agencies issue RFPs or requests for proposals, inviting prospective contractors to submit a written plan describing how the contractor proposes to satisfy the government's requirement as described in the RFP.

lesser part of proposal success than are marketing and negotiating skills. In fact, negotiating skill is properly a part of sales and marketing skills, and it should be recognized as essential to success. However, in those cases where proposals are required, by far the bulk of the task of winning contracts falls on the effectiveness of the proposal, which, if successful, leads to negotiation—but only if successful, which means if the government finds the proposed plan viable and the cost acceptable.

> Success in winning government procurements in which the client requests proposals depends heavily on the sales skills of the contenders. The proposal represents a high peak in the art of sales and marketing skills.

That raises a point that appears to be not always recognized by those writing proposals: The proposal does not normally lead directly to a contract, except in the case of the rather small contract, and should not be expected to do so. The successful proposal leads to negotiation, often via a request for a best and final offer (BAFO). So there is a logic to the remark often made by a client to a *proposal consultant*, "Don't worry about winning the contract. Just get me to the table, and I will take it from there." That client is confident of his or her own negotiating skill, and recognizes that the direct objective of the

 proposal consultant one who offers a special service of sales consulting, helping clients create proposals and/or train their own staffs in proposal writing.

proposal ought to be to win a place at the negotiating table. That consideration alone should dictate the objective of your major strategy.

> Always remember that the direct purpose of your proposal is to get your client to the negotiating table. Direct your sales skills and stratagems to that end.

Clearing the first hurdle and getting to the negotiating table means that your proposal must have been good enough to get serious consideration, as evidenced by the fact that the client wants to discuss it with you. That is the first step of the negotiation, although the contracting officer will rarely concede that you are in negotiations. (That is part of the officer's negotiating tactics.) But that is the meaning of being asked to visit to discuss your proposal.

> When writing a proposal, consider any stratagem that might inspire the agency to want to discuss your proposal in order to ask specific questions or explore the possibilities suggested by your proposed program. (Identifying possible alternatives, for example, may induce the agency to seek a discussion of those alternatives.)

HOW THE GOVERNMENT PAYS

Most government contracts are for fixed-price projects, although there are contracts under which you would have agreed to an hourly/daily rate or a per work unit (e.g., page) rate for certain tasks. Usually, the invitation to submit a proposal or a bid will make clear what kind of contract and payment plan the government proposes to use, but often the agency will invite you to suggest an alternative arrangement if you wish.

PROPOSALS ARE A SPECIAL OPPORTUNITY

In my view, and in the view of others who actually enjoy writing or, at least, do not dislike doing so, the proposal is a very special sales opportunity. But many independent consultants and other independent professionals are reluctant to write proposals, and some simply refuse to do so, thereby foreclosing most opportunities to pursue and win government contracts. That refusal to write proposals may be because they dislike writing (a surprising number of well-educated professionals fall into this category), or because they rebel at the expense of writing proposals. Or perhaps they firmly believe that they are more effective in winning business when they make personal sales calls and presentations, and they reject all less direct approaches to selling than face-to-face presentations and discussions.

On the other hand, there are many consultants who thoroughly dislike cold selling—making sales calls upon strangers and attempting to arouse their interest in what you have to sell. Many even dislike all face-to-face sales contact. For them, advertising, brochures, word of mouth, and proposals are welcome alternatives to personal calls.

ADVANTAGES PROPOSALS OFFER

There are a number of great advantages you enjoy in offering a prospective client a written sales presentation that we call a proposal. Here are a few to think about:

✔ You have ample leisure to think out your many alternatives of program design, explanation, and arguments, giving you the opportunity to help the client understand your reasoning in designing a custom program for him or her.

✔ You can make as many tries at getting it right as you wish—changes, reversals, rewrites, new ideas, old ideas, twists on old ideas, graphic illustrations, and so on as far as your time and patience permit.

✔ You can have others review your drafts and make comments, criticisms, and suggestions, even as devil's advocates.

✔ You can do research as you write, and introduce arguments and examples from as many other sources as you wish or have time to find.

✔ You can take the time to use the creative process described in Chapter 6 to develop new and better ideas.

✔ You can enjoy the benefit of developing a flowchart (see discussion later in this chapter) to help you analyze the client's requirement and plan the solution.

✔ The client has a permanent record of your sales presentation, to read and reread, to study closely, to share with colleagues, and to solicit others' opinions.

✔ You need not ever ruefully comment to yourself or to others, after mentally reviewing a sales presentation you recently made, "I should have said . . ." because you have ample opportunity to review and revise what you said before you finalize and submit your proposal.

The proposal is not a distasteful chore; instead it is a very special opportunity for the preparation of your most powerful sales presentation. Rarely do you have a better opportunity to exercise your most effective sales skills.

In short, in writing a proposal, you have the time and a no-pressure environment to try out many ideas and to revise and polish them extensively, things you cannot do to a great extent in any other kind of presentation, especially not when making a face-to-face oral presentation. In fact, successful proposals are generally those that have been subjected to the processes described. They are what make a properly prepared proposal a powerful sales instrument. Proposal writing is largely an art that depends on your sales skills and, especially, on your creative imagination and capacity for inventiveness. (See Chapter 6 for discussion of creativity.)

PROPOSAL WRITING IN GENERAL

The proposal is a sine qua non for responding to most custom requirements of government agencies, but a great many organizations in the private sector, especially those that are familiar with doing business with the government, are also requesting proposals from consultants today. However, even if a prospective client does not specifically require you to submit a proposal when seeking to select a consultant for award of a contract, asking the client to accept a proposal from you is usually an excellent idea for all the reasons listed earlier. Although this discussion of proposal preparation as a powerful sales tool is cast in the framework of government contracting, what is said here has equal power in selling anything, anywhere, to anyone.

There is a hazard, though, in suggesting to a client the benefits of being able to review a proposal in evaluating candidates for a contract award: It may cause the client to increase the competition by publishing a general request for proposals. Therefore, you must have confidence in your ability to write a powerful proposal and be fully prepared to devote the time and make the considerable effort to writing such a proposal.

> Proposals are used increasingly in contracting in the private sector, with advantages to both client and consultant.

FLOWCHARTING

The flowchart is a powerful, perhaps the most powerful, sales tool in the right hands, because it is a planning tool, a key to analyzing a requirement and designing the most direct and efficient program to satisfy the requirement. As such, it is also a key to accurate estimating of costs because it defines the tasks to be performed, each of which can be costed, taking most of the guesswork out of defining and costing the project to be proposed. (See Chapter 4.) For example, a prospective client invites proposals for creating a direct mail sales campaign. Let us first list the major steps or functions that you would have to identify or create for any such program:

1. Item(s) to be offered.

2. The literature package to mail out.

3. Test program(s).

4. Mailing lists.

5. Fulfillment.

You will have to depend on the client's description of his or her requirement to identify the items more closely. For example, what item or items will be offered? Only the client can define that, and you will need information from the client on all the items. But let us assume that the RFP provides enough detail for each of the items. You might sketch the first rough flowchart along the lines of Figure 8.1.

Each of the steps can be flowcharted to identify each task needed to carry out the step. The first step, for exam-

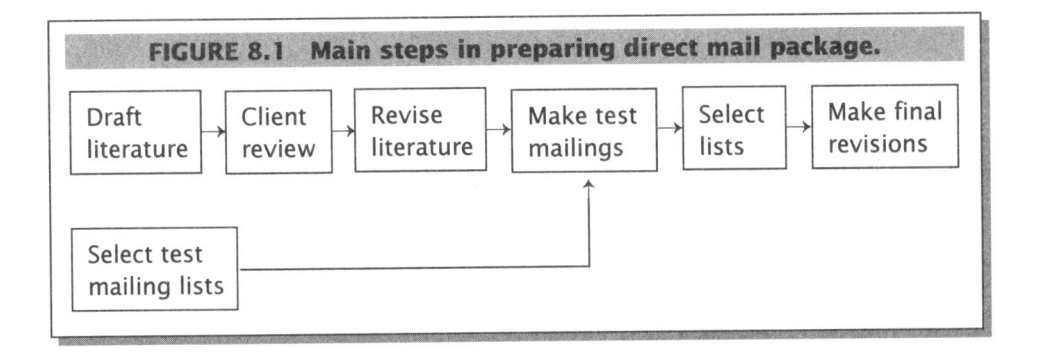

FIGURE 8.1 Main steps in preparing direct mail package.

ple, includes preparing a number of items that are considered to be obligatory in direct mail:

Sales letter.

Brochure.

Order form.

Response envelope.

Most direct mail packages include more than these four items. However, between what the client's RFP stated as details of the client's requirement and what you perceive as necessary, you can chart the development of the package, and you can do the same for each item in the package. Depending on how you see it, you might develop the top-level flowchart first, and then follow it with flowcharts of each item that will require a development process of its own, or you may cover it all in one large flowchart. (I would favor flowcharting each element of the package, at least in rough draft, to minimize the possibility of overlooking some important details, but you or the client may have other ideas.) As an alternative, you might present a development process for each item as a textual list of things to be done in sequence, with relevant discussions. The advantage of flowcharting each major step is, however, greater assurance that you will not miss accounting for any critical tasks in totaling up the labor required and getting an accurate estimate of your costs.

Once you have drafted the flowchart(s), you can draw up a list of items, defining each one quantitatively, and estimate the labor required and any other costs needed to carry out each task. For example, suppose you were to break down the first block, "Draft literature," as follows:

- ✔ Sales letter, three pages.
- ✔ Brochure, 6 × 9, four sides.
- ✔ Order form, 4 × 6, two sides.

Estimate your labor and/or other costs associated with developing the first draft of each item. Bear in mind that the flowcharts must go through the rough draft and revision process, the flowchart revisions being dependent on and inspired by revisions to the text descriptions. Ergo, do not attempt to draw flowcharts in final form until you are satisfied with your text.

The flowcharts and any other material you develop to document your offer in detail have a most important function of minimizing risk, including the risk of unreasonable client demands and client misinterpretation of your contract. Note the importance of quantitatively documenting the tasks and products identified in the flowcharting process, for your proposal is part of your contract. (Be sure that is clearly established by referencing the proposal in the contract.) Specifications must be quantitative, as well as qualitative, to be fully useful. As long as the specifications are quantitative you have the protection that specifications afford you.

Special Items

Items that require special attention in a direct response mailing campaign include, as one of the most important items, the guarantee offered the recipient of the package. It is usual in such campaigns to find the guarantee repeated throughout the literature package as a constant assurance to the recipient. Pay close attention to this in developing your flowcharts and associated texts.

BASIC PRINCIPLES

Creativity has been mentioned in these pages, especially with regard to the marketing functions (e.g., USPs and proposals). You have also read in Chapter 6 discussions of positioning, building your professional image, and getting attention. These three ideas are related to each other and to creativity, and to implement them effectively calls for a degree of boldness and courage. But there is another important point to make about sales presentations in general and proposals in particular. It is this: Proposals and other sales presentations fall into either of two categories with regard to the image they paint of the presentation. Every presentation is in what I call the "Me too" or the "Why me" category. That is, either it says, "I am conventional and conservative, but I do it better than anyone else," or it says, "I have a better idea, especially for you."

There are pros and cons to each approach because there are clients who want the conservative, conventional approach (it seems safer and more likely to work), and there are clients to whom new and different ideas are appealing. There are also consultants who fall into those same two categories, and that is reflected clearly in the proposals and other sales presentations (including logos, slogans, and USPs) they offer. In practice, then, it is not surprising that conservative and conventional approaches are far more evident in all sales materials than are those novel or different ideas.

Note that the client may or may not be the individual who wrote the request for proposals, the individual with whom you visited originally, or the one whose name appears in the request for proposals as the project manager of the effort. It may be a committee or it may be an entire staff of Monday morning quarterbacks expressing their opinions. They may sneer at "the same tired, old methods," or jeer at "new, crackpot ideas."

Admittedly, pursuing the bolder approach of offering new and different approaches to satisfying whatever the client expresses as a need is an immediate hazard and is more likely to draw criticism than is the conservative approach. There is a middle course, fortunately, one that has been used successfully many times. It is using the "better idea" approach, but taking steps to assure the client that it involves no hazard and demonstrating that effectively as a fact.

The key to doing this is to show that the new idea is not revolutionary but is a logical outgrowth of proven methods. Proposing a new "failure analysis" to support a maintenance program, the proposal writer explained that this new idea was based on a logical extension of a conventional "reliability analysis" program. Showing the origins of the better idea as highly respectable and accepted ideas lends credibility and authority, while stressing "new" and "better."

OTHER OPPORTUNITIES IN REGARD TO GOVERNMENT CONTRACTS

Admittedly, the opportunities for contracting with government agencies as a sales consultant are likely to be relatively limited. However, among the many millions of businesses large and small in the United States are a great many who do or want to do business with the governments. Therein is a substantial market for the independent sales consultant. These others, large and small, need help in pursuing and winning government contracts. Some are totally unfamiliar with the government markets and need guidance or specific help. Some do not have staff capabilities for carrying out the marketing chores necessary to winning government contracts, and will retain consultants to help. And some are simply unaware that they can win in government markets until an independent consultant explains the practical possibilities to them. Thus the larger market opportunity for an independent sales consultant lies in serving the needs of others who do or wish to do business with the government. And there is an array of needs to satisfy and services to offer these prospects.

CONTRACTING AS A WAY OF DOING BUSINESS

Many businesses involve formal or informal contracting. In fact, technically, all business involves contracting because any sale includes a contract, even if it is implied, rather than formal. Thus most independent consultants are also independent contractors (ICs), although they may not sign formal contract agreements but rather work on verbal or implied contracts. Thus a sale, for many companies, is represented by a contract negotiated successfully. And so a sales consultant may be a specialist in supporting clients pursuing contracts, whether they are contracts with government agencies or contracts with organizations in the private sector. In fact, that is the consulting specialty I practice, although I selected a special niche in the broad field of sales consulting: I was a proposal specialist, but included a number of related functions in the services I provided my clients.

> As an independent consultant you are also an independent contractor (IC), for clients normally retain you under a contract, whether that is a written document or a verbal agreement.

In fact, the selection of clients who seek help in pursuing and winning contracts is too broad a field for an individual to pursue without specializing. It would be all but impossible to provide effective support for every possible contractor under every possible set of circumstances. Specializing is necessary, and may be along a variety of lines, usually depending on your own experience and fields with which you are familiar. For example:

- ✔ Clients offering some special category of services or products (e.g., moviemaking, electronic devices, and security services).
- ✔ Clients pursuing certain special kinds of customers and contracts, such as government contracts or maintenance contracts.
- ✔ Clients that are small businesses.
- ✔ Clients that are large corporations.
- ✔ Clients needing only certain special categories of support services, such as proposal writing, market research, and needs analysis.

> Imagination and innovation are important elements in every independent consultant's set of skills and utilities. There is always a better way to overcome a problem, design a system, or make an important point. Train yourself in creative thinking and use it to develop new ideas.

One mind-set that helps you in keeping a proper orientation for such thinking is forgetting, for the moment, that your (your client's) ultimate goal in writing a proposal is to win a contract. Concentrate your attention on the more immediate goal of getting your client to the table, where he or she can exercise his or her own sales skills and business judgment. Ergo, your proposal strategy should include focus on some stratagem that will motivate the client's prospect to request a meeting to ask questions and discuss your proposal. If the client's prospect is so impressed by your offer as to wish to go directly to negotiations, well and good. However, anything in your proposal that arouses the interest of your client's prospect enough to want a meeting and discussion is a first-step victory in itself. It is a great help, even if the client's prospect is merely curious and wishes to ask you (your client) some questions; it is an important step forward toward the ultimate goal. Aiming to have something in your presentation that raises questions or special interest in the prospect's mind is a possible strategic orientation.

> Getting your client to the table is itself a successful proposal outcome. Therefore, make that goal an important part of your proposal strategy.

There are, of course, many lines in which one may specialize, and we will discuss and exemplify a few of these as we proceed. Clients who need sales and marketing help to win contracts are candidates for a variety of services you may wish to offer. Here are a few typical ones that I have personally found many clients welcoming when offered:

- ✔ Market research, identifying suitable sales opportunities.
- ✔ Preparing proposals and/or related sales materials.
- ✔ Needs analysis of clients requesting proposals, identifying best strategies, offering recommendations.
- ✔ Training staffs in suitable sales techniques, market research, and proposals.
- ✔ Doing the legwork, acting as the client's representative or agent.
- ✔ Accompanying the client to and assisting the client at the negotiating table.
- ✔ Protesting some aspect of a procurement.
- ✔ Advising clients generally in procurement matters.

You might offer all of these services to your clients if you feel confident that you can handle all of them with equal skill and success, although restricting yourself to the kinds of clients or kinds of contracts you wish to make your specialty. There are sales consultants who claim only one or two of these services as their specialties, although they may offer all to their clients. They thus offer a broad service, but still retain the image of specialization. Ideally, the terms by which you explain and identify your specialty should include the benefit you offer your clients. For example, while I am known as a proposal specialist or proposal writer, I always include the motto or slogan "I help clients win contracts" in publicizing my service, thereby pointing out and stressing the benefit.

> Even if you actually provide a wide set of services to your clients, keep a focus on one or two (preferably one) that represents (and clearly explains) your professional specialty in terms of benefit to your clients.

One important thing to note: While it is both necessary and helpful to be fully familiar with how government agencies and organizations in private industry contract for goods and services, be clear in your mind that there is a broad distinction between how the various organizations buy and how to sell to them. In other words, how an organization buys and how you must sell to it are two different subjects, and you must understand the distinction. The client follows some set of rules or guidelines in his or her purchasing, and you must understand those; but it is up to you to bring to bear all the strategies and techniques of selling that you believe to be most persuasive in drawing the client to the table. That, I have found, often demands that you invent new approaches and offer new and different ideas that make your own proposal a standout from the crowd in both commanding attention and presenting an offer the client will be hard-pressed to refuse.

RESEARCHING GOVERNMENT MARKETS

You need to know how to find opportunities in government markets, if you are to base some of your work on government purchasing. The *Commerce Business Daily* was pointed to earlier as a source of information. Today, the *CBD* is both a print publication and an electronic one. The Loren Data Corporation publishes the *CBD* on its web site at www.ld.com/cbd/today/ every business day, but the *CBD* is also available elsewhere on the Internet. The following two Internet addresses offer many leads to federal government procurement information and assistance:

> The Federal Acquisition Jumpstation: nais.nasa.gov/fedproc/home.html.
>
> Department of Commerce: cbdnet.access.gpo.gov/index.html.

For state and local government announcements of procurement needs and guidance, go to www.fedmarket.com/sales_resources/bids/state_local.html#1.

This is a starter list. New web sites spring up almost daily. These URLs will lead you to many other locations with additional information on government markets, probably far more information than you need or can use; but you will gain an appreciation of the size and scope of government purchasing.

The various government levels of the United States are as firmly committed to e-commerce—doing business in cyberspace via the Internet and the World Wide Web—as are so many private sector business organizations. The benefits accrue as much to you as a supplier as they do to the government as a buyer.

Chapter 9

Ancillary Services and Other Income Sources

There is more than one medium and method for delivering useful and appropriate consulting services to clients, with resulting benefits to both client and consultant.

WHY ANCILLARY SERVICES AND OTHER INCOME SOURCES?

Independent consultants normally supply their services in at least three working modes: as independent contractor, as subcontractors, and as temporary staff. In these modes, consultants may work on the client's premises, on the consultant's own premises, or on both. In each of these modes, the consultant practices his or her consulting specialties in direct support of the client. (That is, the consultants do more than advise. The engineering consultant does engineering, the computer programming consultant programs, the writing consultant writes, etc.)

Unfortunately, there are some shortcomings to these modes of service from both the client's and the consultant's viewpoints. One such shortcoming, for example, is that these modes dictate and limit the conditions under which the client may utilize the consultant's services. Under that limitation, the result is that some individuals who have a need of those support services are unable to use them for any of several reasons, including cost. Thus, both consultant and client have lost.

From your viewpoint as the independent consultant, this points immediately to one of two main reasons for and considerations in diversifying your practice by creating ancillary services such as those to be discussed in this chapter and delivered to clients via printed texts, lectures, tapes (audio and video), e-mail, and even telephone. One major problem is that independent consulting tends strongly to be a feast-or-famine enterprise, with peaks of work too great for you to handle, and valleys of idleness that wreak havoc with your annual income. There is rarely a way to store overloads of demand and satisfy them later when things are slower, so you must pass overloads on to someone else or simply decline the assignments and lose the fruit of your marketing investment.

Developing other income centers helps greatly in leveling the average work load, filling in some of the valleys and lending flexibility in handling peaks of demand. Overloads of demand are normally not under your control, not even to a small extent; they occur when they occur, and you can only react to them. There are other recommended activities described in this chapter, however, that are under your control and that you can manage in ways to help even out your workload and keep you gainfully employed throughout the year.

From the accounting viewpoint, keeping you gainfully employed is maximizing your billable hours. You bill your time spent on providing ancillary services to an internal account of your practice. This not only keeps your overhead expense under control, but it also provides an accounting of the costs of each ancillary service and enables you to determine what each contributes to your consulting practice.

Another compelling reason for adding these ancillary services to your agenda is that, aside from contributing income to your practice and helping flatten the curves a bit, the ancillary activities referred to and discussed in this chapter are themselves consulting services, logical parts of a complete consulting services package. They are additional modes of serving your clients by complementing those obvious and traditional consulting services delivered personally by you in the classic face-to-face work environment. They thus make your practice a much more complete array of relevant and appropriate consulting services, and help you provide consulting services to clients who could not otherwise afford them.

A broad array of services also supports your marketing in general by raising your visibility and enhancing your professional image as the provider of a complete consulting service. In fact, that characteristic of being a complete package from which a client may select the most appropriate services is an excellent basis for the creation of one or more compelling USPs. (See Chapter 6 for relevant USP discussions.)

> Ancillary services provide several benefits, helping fill in valleys in the feast-or-famine consulting business, but also enabling you to reach many more clients and delivering surprise benefits to your marketing program.

ADVANTAGES OF SUCH A COMPLEMENT

The easy availability and convenience of these complementing services and products offer a number of advantages to both you and your clients. In many situations, as noted earlier, some prospective clients may not be able to take advantage of services that are available only on the traditional basis of your full time, personally doing whatever is necessary to satisfy the client's need. That is the most expensive way to utilize consulting services, and there are clients who can't afford and who do not need such intensive support as that personal face-to-face service provides. The alternative consulting services provided by your ancillary programs might deliver modified kinds of consulting, such as virtual group consulting (analogous to the well-known group therapy sessions), at a far smaller cost to each individual client who participates in an ancillary program. At the same time, the program brings you greater income because you provide service to many clients simultaneously with each individual presentation. Moreover, the ancillary programs enable clients to allocate time for consulting help at their convenience and to review what they have learned (some of these methods are learning experiences) and gain more utility from the services.

These alternative services enable you to reach a far greater number of clients, since you now reach out to groups, as well as to individual clients, and you offer your expertise in flexible formats and on flexible schedules to those selected groups of clients (e.g., subscribers, associates, listeners, etc.). I have found it possible also to introduce a good measure of individual counseling by answering questions and giving advice from the lecture platform; in the texts of newsletters, reports, faxes, and e-mail; and via brief telephone conversations. You will be able to perceive the logic of all of this as we proceed.

> The many ancillary ways to deliver useful consulting services to clients enable you to offer a complete consulting service with choices for clients and products you create to support and strengthen your practice.

There are several general categories of the kinds of ancillary services you can create and offer prospective clients. They cover writing for publication by others; publishing your own writings, compact discs, and tapes for direct sale to clients; and speaking publicly, lecturing in formal and informal environments.

These ideas are implemented in a number of ways,

including the following as a starter list from which you can select those that seem most appropriate to you:

- ✔ Newsletters, printed and electronic.
- ✔ An associates program.
- ✔ An information center.
- ✔ Special reports, printed and on compact discs and tapes.
- ✔ Articles in others' periodicals.
- ✔ Books, printed and on discs and tapes.
- ✔ Speaking engagements.
- ✔ Seminars, open.
- ✔ Seminars, custom.
- ✔ Seminars, mini.
- ✔ Formal classes in adult education.
- ✔ Formal classes, custom.

Most of these categories can be singular or plural as to content. That is, you might have more than one seminar, newsletter, and/or special report you can deliver for different kinds of sales promotions. You probably will not want to undertake all these ideas, but the choices are numerous enough for you to select from them whatever you prefer. Following is a brief look at several of the categories.

NEWSLETTERS AND ASSOCIATES PROGRAM

Newsletters and articles used for marketing can be of the conventional printed type—ink on paper—or they can appear in the form of so-called electronic ink (as e-mail or other manifestations in cyberspace). You may not be able to gain income from electronic publication, since Internet users have become accustomed to getting information at no charge on the Net, where most newsletters and other publications are free. You are much more likely to be successful in charging a subscription fee for paper-and-ink newsletters and reports than for electronic versions. You can lend your newsletter two-way communication and a measure of individual consulting by inviting questions from readers and responding to them in your next issue. In my own case, I created an associates program, charging an annual fee that included subscription to the newsletter (although one could subscribe to the newsletter only, and not to the associates program), a package of reports, and the right to several free consultations by mail or telephone. ("Mail" would include e-mail, of course.) I also diversified the content of my newsletters by inviting and publishing guest articles by readers, associates, and other consultants.

I found, in practice, that by far the majority of subscribers opted to join the associates program, in verification of my belief that many, if not most, people like to belong. You can create such a program easily and run it entirely by e-mail, although there are still many millions of people who do not own computers or who, even if they have computers, prefer words printed on paper. That is especially the case if your clients are busy executives, few of whom will take the time to learn and use a PC at their desks (unless they are in the computer business).

The point is that an electronic publication will not reach all the prospects you will want to reach and who will want to read your newsletter and reports. Many individuals, such as corporate executives, neither own nor use a computer, and still rely, by preference, on reading conventional printed material to gain much of their information. On the premise that your sales appeals are going to be directed largely to executives in organizations, it seems wise to publish a paper-and-ink newsletter—possibly with a free electronic version, perhaps in condensed or summary format, in the manner of the *New York Times* and a few others that do exactly that. You will have far less resistance to a subscription fee for an attractive newsletter printed on good-quality paper than you will encounter in trying to persuade "netizens" (people who spend much of their time on the Internet and rely heavily on it for information and communication), and you may be surprised at how well an offer of an associate status will be received by readers if presented properly. Overall, the publishing of a free electronic abstract of your printed newsletter, with some useful information included, provides an excellent marketing tool for selling your printed newsletter and your services in general.

> Despite the great number of visitors to the Internet, there are many millions of good prospects who do not visit cyberspace, and you would miss all these prospects if you relied solely on subscribers to an electronic newsletter. You must therefore consider publishing a conventional printed newsletter.

CREATIVE THINKING

A consultant ought to have an active imagination and pronounced creative instincts, if nothing else. No matter how many ideas you find here and in other reading you do, the best source of useful, new ideas resides between your own ears, and you should encourage your conscious and subconscious minds to quest constantly for new and useful ideas. (See Chapter 6 for discussion of creativity.) Remember in this connection that "new," as in "new idea," is a relative term, for virtually every idea has roots somewhere from which it has sprung. Most often it is a twist on another idea, a better way to do something that needs to be done, so do not be reluctant to consider what are established ideas and quest for better ways to do something. Here is one idea that I found to be profitable and useful. Following an appearance on TV as the guest of a daytime talk show, I was besieged with telephone calls asking me questions. After a few days of this, I conceived the idea of handling this via what I called a "mini-seminar." I had offices in the city at the time, so I arranged to hold the mini-seminar in my office each Saturday afternoon, with an attendance of not more than 25 people. I scheduled it for three hours (although it often ran much longer than that), charged a small fee for attendance, and conducted an informal program in which I delivered a presentation of less than one hour and gave the rest of the time over to questions that I answered, with response invited also from all attendees. It was a highly successful idea.

> A mini-seminar held on Saturdays for a limited number of attendees and at a modest price may fit your program nicely as a source of income and an aid to your marketing.

CONSULTING SERVICES INFORMATION CENTER

As an alternative to an associates program, you may wish to consider establishing an information center, with the array of newsletters, reports, seminars, and all other ancillary activities as elements of the center's program. That term suggests consulting services more than the word "associates" does, although the latter term definitely has a great deal of appeal. Perhaps you could combine the terms, and offer associate status in a consulting services information center.

YOUR OWN SPECIAL NICHE MARKET

Once you build your associates subscription list, you have a very special niche market of your own. (See Chapter 7 for discussion of niche markets.) Those on the list are already your special clients, with whom you are in continuous touch via your newsletter and any other communication you wish to create, and they represent great marketing opportunities as favored clients who are the first to receive any special offers you wish to make. (Be sure that those on your list are made aware of this.) You would do well to create some distinctive logo and letterhead on which to send messages to your associates and make them special offers. Your associates program should include things to offer them frequently throughout the year—reports, books, and other special offers. You may eventually even wish to organize an annual trade show or convention.

SPECIAL REPORTS

All these same principles would apply to any special reports and other writings you choose to publish yourself, as well as to newsletters. Each special report, whatever its length, could be marketed via a free electronic abstract circulated by e-mail, web sites, and whatever other cyberspace routes you can find to utilize. (There are other cyberspace routes, such as newsgroups, chat rooms, and guest articles for newsletters and other publishers of electronic periodicals.) Here are just a few ideas for such reports:

- ✔ Benefits of Direct Response Sales.
- ✔ How to Run a Warehouse Sale.
- ✔ How to Find Out If Your Advertising Works.
- ✔ Ideas for Running "Special Sales."
- ✔ Novel Promotional Ideas.
- ✔ What Is a USP and Why Do You Need One?
- ✔ Running an Auction as a Special Promotion.
- ✔ How to Add Mail Order Gold to Your Marketing.

Other ideas for reports would be suggested by inferring from the kinds of businesses your associates and subscribers are in the subjects that would probably be of special interest to them.

These reports can be of any length—a few pages to a few dozen pages or even more. The benefits can be enormous. An exceptionally good report can create a top-notch reputation for you and bring you a surge of publicity (increased visibility) almost overnight. And like newsletters and all the other ancillary services you might develop and offer, successful reports tend to increase the number of conventional consulting contracts you are offered.

> Main reasons for offering ancillary services were given at the beginning of this chapter, but another reason is an unexpected benefit: These services work directly to bring in new clients for your classic consulting services at whatever rates you normally charge for your time and efforts.

SPIN-OFF BENEFITS OF YOUR SPECIAL REPORTS

There is a special way to use your reports (and your newsletter and lecture presentations, too, for that matter) to expand and add to your services. Write at least some of your reports and newsletter articles to explore new ideas and reader interests. When you find that something you wrote about generates an especially great amount of interest or enthusiasm from readers, you may have gotten a clue to a service niche or niche program (see Chapter 7). In this way, you can use some of your ancillary activities as marketing tools, uncovering clients' needs and wants of which you have not been aware—you had no way to be aware of them—and actually create new and unique markets for your services. That, the creation of your own niche markets, is a most welcome new meaning of the word "independent." You will have leaped ahead of your competitors with a giant stride!

WRITING SELL COPY

Despite the fact that selling consulting services effectively usually requires a special approach to marketing, it also still requires many of the same kinds of marketing tools that other sales programs require. Marketing in general depends on printed literature to perhaps a larger degree than most of us realize. With all the modern miracles of communication, and despite the rise of e-commerce, it is still necessary to place in a client's hand something tangible in sales literature, some written copy, as a record and ready reference. Most of us who are not directly involved in the process do not think of the fact that someone must write the copy for all sales and marketing literature, and that all of it must be *sell copy* to be effective.

What Is Sell Copy?

The written and printed materials upon which marketing depends so heavily exist in a wide variety of forms, and the list includes at least the following well-known written sales tools: business cards, sales letters, brochures, pamphlets, catalog sheets, specifications, item descriptions, flyers, broadsides, manuals, card mailers, proposals, advertisements, magazine articles, publicity releases, and invoice stuffers.

 sell copy anything written to sell something; copywriting.

All of these represent what is referred to here as sell copy, copy that is intended to motivate the reader to buy the product. It is persuasive copy, the kind of literature designed primarily to convince prospects to become customers— to buy what is described and offered. Some of them are direct sell—sales letters, brochures, and proposals, for example—which exhort the reader to order the item or items immediately; others are indirect sell, supporting the direct sell pieces and encouraging the reader to take some important next step toward making a purchase, without including the actual exhortation to buy. Direct sell, however, is usually not a practicable marketing approach for selling consulting services. It simply does not work well, with only rare exceptions. And so we will consider sell copy here only as it applies to selling sales consulting services.

Sales Letters

The sales letter is probably the most common and most frequently used sales tool. It is used in several ways and in several situations, but there are only two applications that seem to have value here:

1. Response to an inquiry.
2. Special announcement.

Response to an Inquiry. One almost automatic use of the sales letter is as the natural response to an inquiry. A client or prospective client writes or calls to inquire about something, and the consultant responds with a tactful sales letter, explaining the benefits and features of the services and, possibly, quoting prices accordingly. This kind of sales letter is written individually and on a custom basis to the prospect, although the marketer may have some standard form or format to use as the basis for the letter.

Special Announcement. A second possible use of the sales letter is to make a special announcement (usually a special offer) to clients and others on the in-house mailing lists. Most of us get such letters occasionally from department stores whose credit cards we use. This is a mass-produced form letter, of course, since it is sent out in quantity to an entire mailing list of some kind. It is usually futile to send out your special announcement to a mailing list of strangers, and so the mailing list ought to be of clients and former clients or, at least, of prospective clients who know of you and what you do.

Brochures

The word "brochure" is a most general term and is often defined in dictionaries as a sewn document, since the word comes from the French *brocher*, to sew. In reality it refers to a wide variety of ways and end products in which the idea of a brochure is implemented, from the simple sheet folded once or twice to the formally bound—even sewn—publication. Examples of sales tools considered to be brochures vary from an $8^1/_2$-by-11-inch sheet folded into six panels and suitable to fit into a number 10 business envelope to 9-by-12-inch documents that are thick with many pages. Brochures vary in size and cost, from the inexpensive and simple to the costly and fancy, as well as in basic method, over an almost unimaginably wide range. Perhaps many of the little documents considered to be brochures are more accurately described as pamphlets, and some of the more elaborate examples as booklets, but the distinctions are of little practical significance: The intent of every brochure is to make a presentation.

Proposals

Proposals have been discussed earlier (Chapter 8) as an important marketing tool, but it is an added income source if you sell services to help clients with their proposals. (For some consultants, proposal support represents their full-time practice.) Depending on the nature and size of the contract and the typical practices in the relevant industry, proposals range from being largely boilerplated, even including the seller's standard brochures and specifications, to being a totally custom-written product. (Most references to proposals in these pages are to those proposals that are completely custom written.) They may also vary from a few pages each to thick volumes of hundreds of pages and to more than one volume, à la some elaborate and expensive proposals written by major defense contractors in pursuit of multimillion-dollar defense contracts. (Not surprisingly, the size of the proposal is usually in some proportion to the size of the contract being pursued.)

ARTICLES IN OTHER PERIODICALS AND BOOKS

There are many periodicals published by others in which the articles have been written by people such as yourself—contributors. Some periodicals pay contributors for their contributions, but many contributors are well satisfied to be rewarded by the publicity or recognition they gain in being formally published. These periodicals can vary from journals published by associations of various kinds, to trade magazines circulated within some trade or profession, to commercial magazines sold on newsstands. I have known of some practitioners who won new business as a result of having written a letter to the editor that was published in a periodical, for example. Some contributors have their articles collected and reprinted in a volume, even as a self-published book, and use copies as direct mailing pieces.

Books are an important category. Being the author of a published book tends to lend you a special prestige as a consulting expert. Some practitioners self-publish their books, but having your book published by a mainstream book publisher whose name is well known is far more prestigious and relieves you of the burdensome problems and costs of marketing the book.

If a book of which you are the author meets with great success in the marketplace (i.e., if it sells in great numbers) your name becomes well known in relevant circles, not only as the author of the book, but as an expert in the subject of the book. The resultant publicity and enhanced reputation can lead to many other books, speaking engagements, and consulting assignments, and a great increase in your prestige as a consultant expert. That latter, a marked increase in your prestige, usually results in significant increases in your consulting rates.

PUBLIC SPEAKING

Speaking before groups—"on the platform"—and on radio and TV offers a wealth of new opportunities. A great many consulting assignments result both directly and indirectly from public speaking activities. That is, in many cases—more often than not, in fact—people hearing you speak call later to discuss their needs and often then retain you. But even when none of those in your audiences call, public speaking usually brings you added business ultimately because you become more widely known as a specialist and expert in your field of sales. You will benefit from the quite surprising phenomena of achieving enhanced prestige as an expert overnight and of being recommended to clients by those who know of you only by your reputation, but are satisfied that you are whatever that reputation claims for you.

Often, someone who is impressed with you and your reputation, but has himself or herself no need for your services, will recommend you highly to others. One way and another, others hear of you and call on you for whatever you sell. In fact, there have been cases where I was one of several speakers addressing an audience and another speaker on the program retained me to do some work for a company. This has been true even when I have been paid a substantial fee for speaking, although I have also often chosen to make presentations without direct compensation, charging my time to my own marketing budget. That latter measure is a quite proper thing to do, and has proved a most profitable idea in terms of marketing results.

Be sure to make something with your name and directions for reaching you—a card or brochure of some kind—readily available to all in any audience you address.

Public speaking is as broad a category as is writing and publishing. It includes delivering seminars, organized classes, lectures, and speeches in both formal and informal settings. For example, you may be asked to offer your remarks to a meeting of some local association, and that alone can bring you new clients. Or you may be asked to speak more formally at a local college or a national convention. That, too, is a marketing asset that can bring you a satisfactory fee . On the other hand, you may very well be expected to speak without a fee at meetings of local groups or in other informal circumstances. Still, even that can be a productive marketing activity, if you are satisfied to speak for the sake of the added exposure (publicity) and the rewards that may bring.

Unfortunately, you may be like many individuals who have platform allergies. The mere thought of speaking to an assemblage of people—of being the center of attention—causes your palms to sweat and gives you hot flashes, weakness in your knees, and butterflies in your stomach. There are some professional speakers and entertainers who never get over this, but simply learn to force themselves to mount the dais each time. In most cases, the symptoms subside and disappear as soon as you start to talk and warm to your subject and your audience. Or you may adjust completely, eventually, and never again be troubled by these symptoms. Either way, you can learn to be an effective public speaker, just as I and countless others did when we first forced ourselves to climb the steps to the dais, smile, and start talking. (In my case, it was the U.S. Army that forced me to learn how to deliver lectures to assembled groups, and pass on to the troops what I had learned in the special schools I had attended on patrolling, mines, booby traps, explosives, demolitions, and sundry other delightful military specialties in violent aggressiveness.)

Perhaps the underlying reason for platform fright is the mistaken notion that a public speaker requires special skills and talents. The fact is that many professional speakers and performers do have special skills, acquired through training, long practice, and unknown sources such as genetics. Sometimes these were built on a foundation of some natural assets, such as a remarkable speaking voice (the late actor Richard Burton, for example, had such a voice), some instinctive talent for speaking publicly, or perhaps some blessed lack of fear or natural extroversion. But those are exceptional circumstances, and it is certainly not necessary to have such special talents, training, or extroversion to be a successful speaker. A great many nonprofessional speakers are extremely effective and successful on the platform. Some even have speech impediments; many have raspy, thin, or nasal voices; and others are guilty of all the sins that horrify professional speech coaches, such as swallowing their consonants and muffling their vowels.

The fact is that you require no special talents to be a public speaker. Even a rasping or grating voice cannot prevent you from succeeding if you have some rather simple qualifications:

1. Something to say—something that audiences will find worth listening to.
2. Sincere interest in and affection for people generally and for your audience especially.
3. Genuine interest in communicating the information to an audience of listeners.
4. Great enthusiasm for your subject.

The late popular singer Nat "King" Cole revealed in an interview that early in his career he had been given a most valuable tip by the great entertainer Cab Calloway. Cole said that Calloway urged him to articulate the words of the lyrics clearly when he sang so that everyone in his audience could hear and understand every word. Cole, of course, did so, as you can easily verify when listening to one of his records. The advice was excellent and applies even more importantly to public speaking. Whether your voice is remarkably good or not, your audience must be able to understand exactly what you are saying. Your listeners will forgive and soon not even hear any raspiness, hoarseness, or other faulty characteristic of your voice if they hear and understand clearly and are interested in what you are saying, If nothing else, make sure that they can do so.

The real trick is to be prepared. That does not mean to have a memorized speech. That usually comes across as a dull mechanical reading. It takes an expert actor to deliver a memorized speech and make it appear to be spontaneous. Being prepared, however, means knowing your subject thoroughly so that you can make even extemporaneous statements smoothly and without hesitation, respond to questions immediately and fluently, and meet challenges from your audience with a smile and quiet, self-confident response. (Do not polarize things by arguing vociferously or embarrassing your challenger, even if you could easily do so. Be diplomatic and objective or at least appear to be open-minded in responding, but never embarrass anyone before the audience.) There is no good substitute for being a true expert in your subject, able to think on your feet. If you know your subject thoroughly, your audience will soon recognize that, and if you do not know your subject thoroughly, your audience will soon perceive that as a fact.

Audiences always respond to the speaker who is truly interested in them and likes them. You can't conceal it, and you can't fake it. Audiences pick up immediately on sham interest and cynicism. Obvious enthusiasm for your subject is especially effective. Enthusiasm—*your* enthusiasm—captivates an audience. They feel it, and they are turned on by it, if it is sincere. You can no more fake enthusiasm than you can fake anything else. An audience has an uncanny ability to see through phoniness; you must believe in what you are presenting if you want your listeners to believe in it. That is far more important than oratorical polish. (Corollary: Choose subjects about which you are enthusiastic and in which you are highly knowledgeable or can make yourself knowledgeable through research, as discussed in Chapter 12.)

SEMINARS

Seminars are an increasingly popular means of delivering and gaining special information. (See Chapter 7 also for discussion of seminars.) In the most classical or traditional sense, a seminar is a meeting of graduate students with a professor to discuss and explore research problems. But that meaning has long been lost by extension in this modern world, where both presenting and attending seminars have become a popular and necessary commercial activity. This is largely a result of an increasingly complex world.

In today's world it is almost impossible, in most career fields, to be a generalist if you are to be recognized and effective as an expert. We are compelled to specialize. However, it is increasingly difficult to do even that today, for what is a specialty today becomes an impossibly generalized field tomorrow, forcing a subdivision into more specialties. One who was a specialist yesterday often finds that he or she is today a generalist within a specialized field. Each new development further fragments the field. In electronics, for example, which became a formal course of education in colleges only after World War II, continuous advances split the broad field into such specialties as computers, communications, avionics, satellites, radar, audio, radio, television, microwave equipment, mobile radio, and others. Each of these categories soon expanded to develop its own specialties, and those continued to fragment. The problem is found in many other fields as well. The physician for whom surgery was a specialty yesterday today finds that it is difficult to be a generalist as a surgeon; surgeons specialize in brain surgery, heart transplants, or other special applications. The lawyer who specialized in trial law continues to be a specialist by restricting his or her trial practice to some specific class of trials. The computer programmer of yesterday no longer programs in all the possible languages or to satisfy all kinds of needs, but is proficient and specializes in certain computer languages, machines, and/or kinds of software. Merely to keep up with your own specialty in fields where almost anything more than a year old is already obsolescent is a problem in itself.

That is the kind of problem a great many seminars are designed to solve, for the seminar is usually a highly specialized, highly concentrated, and relatively brief training session focused sharply on a single specialized subject, which is itself often a new development. Seminars vary in length from about a half-day to a week (five days), but most last from one to three days.

Seminar Subjects

Subject matter of seminars varies quite widely. This is not surprising, considering that seminars normally deal in highly specialized subjects. You might develop seminars in the design of sales promotion, in direct response sales, in warehouse sales, or in any other sales specialty.

Typically, seminars are held in hotel meeting rooms, although they may be conducted anywhere—in a university classroom, in a conference room, even in a meeting room of a public library, or wherever a group may be gathered and seated. And groups vary widely in size, from as few as 10 to as many as 200, with the typical or average size probably between 30 and 60 attendees.

Seminars for Profit

For many, seminar presentation has become a business in itself, an income-producing activity on a regular basis. There are organizations that produce or sponsor seminars regularly, usually with a special arrangement for providing the staff or faculty. In most cases such organizations make arrangements with some expert in the field, such as yourself, to design and develop a seminar program and to present it on a fee basis or, quite often, on a profit-sharing basis with a guarantee of some minimum fee. A one-day seminar is likely to have a single presenter and a longer seminar to have a staff of several presenters or a principal presenter/host with a number of guest speakers.

Such seminars generally include handouts of some

sort—often a complete manual, sometimes a relevant commercially published book (which may be a book written by the principal presenter)—and audiovisual aids.

Seminar Economics

If you wish to offer a seminar to the general public, you will have to consider the usual expense of organizing and presenting a public seminar on your own. Following is a list of items of expense, in descending order of magnitude:

1. Advertising to attract attendees: printed notices, mailing, posters, press releases, other.
2. Labor fees: your own direct labor and that of any others who help.
3. Rental of the meeting room.
4. Refreshments.
5. Presentation materials and equipment: slides, chalkboard, transparencies, and so on.
6. Handouts.

Perhaps the easiest way to put others' seminars to good use in your own service and to learn the seminar business is to offer to appear at a seminar for which the sponsor or producer marshals a staff of several presenters. Each presenter is given from perhaps 15 minutes to a full hour to present his or her material. At seminars and meetings of this type there is usually a literature table in the back of the room, and each presenter is free to deposit there his or her own sales literature and business cards. Make it clear to the audience, when you speak at one of these kinds of events, that your cards and literature are on the table, and be sure that they can identify which are yours (i.e., make your identity absolutely clear).

You may get paid for making such presentations as a guest speaker, although a great many presenters appear sans fee or honorarium of any kind, either as an act of noblesse oblige or for the marketing value of the appearance. In fact, many companies maintain an in-house speakers bureau for the express purpose of providing speakers (without charge) on subjects relevant to the company's industry. It is an integral part of the company's marketing department and *public relations (PR)* program. Usually, most of the executives of the company are listed as speakers, and are available to speak to various groups and at various occasions, as requested. Even as a one-person speakers bureau you will find many groups eager to accept your offer to speak at their gatherings if you send out a letter describing the subjects on which you offer to speak and the amount of advance notice you require.

The seminar at which you speak may be part of a convention or a completely separate event. In either case, feel free to move about and mingle with attendees and visitors, especially at large conventions, and meet people. Carry an ample supply of business cards and some kind of brochure small enough to fit in one's pocket or purse. This kind of marketing may pay off even more handsomely than the seminar presentation.

Many organizations will retain you to deliver your seminars to their own staffs, at whatever fees you can negotiate. This is, of course, a way to present seminars at zero risk because you have no expense except travel (which is reimbursed). Instead of marketing your seminar to the public, you market it to organizations. Organizations with several offices will often retain you to present your seminar at each of their offices, and large organizations will sometimes want you to present your seminar individually to each of their departments.

public relations (PR) activities to maintain an individual's or organization's visibility and image at most desirable levels; also referred to as publicity.

OTHER PUBLIC SPEAKING

Most communities of size have adult education courses conducted by at least one junior college or even a full four-year college. Such programs are usually receptive to proposals for new courses, and they pay instructors some kind of tuition fee. Delivering such a course is an easy activity—the classes tend to be small and conducted in the evening.

There are many speakers bureaus whose business it is to provide professional speakers and entertainers for their clients. Their clients are organizations that seek to book speakers for special events, and the bureaus help them identify the kind of speakers they want and find those speakers for them. Many of the speakers such bureaus place are public figures who command very large speaking fees by virtue of their celebrity, and a few are entertainers, but the majority are full-time professional speakers who are registered with many bureaus, speaking professionally almost every day for suitable fees. The publication *Sharing Ideas* (see Chapter 7) and the well-known Dottie Walters, editor of that publication and a leading light in the professional speaking field, will put you in touch with professionals in that industry.

Chapter

10

Contracts and Negotiations

Consulting services are normally contracted for by clients and therefore consultants are usually contractors or subcontractors. Thus consultants are well advised to have a practical understanding of contracts and negotiations.

CONTRACTS AND AGREEMENTS

A contract is necessarily an agreement, but an agreement is not necessarily a contract. That is because to be a contract—an enforceable legal *instrument* —an agreement must meet five requirements:

1. There is an *offer* made by one *party*.
2. There is an *acceptance* of that offer by the other party.
3. There is a *consideration* (money, usually, but not necessarily).
4. The contract is between parties who are fully *competent*.
5. The acts or actions agreed to are within the law.

In certain cases, the law requires that the contract be in written form, as a sixth condition. Otherwise, any agreement meeting the aforementioned five conditions is

instrument
written legal document, such as a will, contract, or deed.

offer
obligatory condition of contracts in which one party makes an offer.

party
one individual or organization entering into a contract.

acceptance
obligatory condition of contracts in which one party accepts the other's offer.

consideration
that which changes hands as payment for exchange, usually paid by the party expressing acceptance of an offer; obligatory element in contracts.

a binding contract, even if not in written form. When people refer to "the contract," they usually mean the written document. However, it is the agreement meeting the above conditions, and not a piece of paper, that is the contract in the eyes of the law.

> To be a legally binding contract, an agreement requires an offer, acceptance, consideration, the parties to be competent, and the agreement to be for some action that is legal. The contract should be in writing, but that is not a legal requirement. There are simple alternatives to document an agreement and make it a legally binding contract.

The popular image of a contract is that of a large number of pages, neatly typed, heavy with "wherefores," "whereases," and "parties of the first part," and bound in a blue folder with ribbons and seals. In fact, there are a number of much simpler ways to enter into a binding contract.

Verbal Contract

Verbal contracts that meet the five conditions stated are legally binding and enforceable. The problem is, of course, that there is no way to verify the original agreement when one must rely on the memories and allegations of the contracting parties, so verbal contracts are of use only when the transaction is so small as not to merit the trouble and cost of preparing even the following simple alternatives to formal written contracts.

> A verbal contract is binding but without a written record of the terms agreed to, it's hard to enforce such a contract.

Purchase Order

One simple alternative that documents the basic agreement in writing is the purchase order. It may be unilateral, simply a form that authorizes you, as the party to whom it is addressed and issued, to perform certain services for a stipulated sum. The purchase order can be as informal as that in Figure 10.1, and usually is when the issuing organization does not use many purchase orders and thus has no need for a special purchase order form suited to its

 competent adult and of normal intelligence; mandatory condition of both parties to make an agreement a legally binding contract.

FIGURE 10.1 A typical purchase order.

Gerry Williams & Co.
Investments
Whitestone Building, Suite 917
San Diego, CA 71989

Purchase Order

Issued to Henry Horner
P.O. Box 17863
Los Angeles, CA 90123

FOR: Development of a 6 x 9 brochure and sales letter for a direct mail sales campaign announcing the opening of the Gerry Williams Investment Services. First draft of each item will be delivered not later than 45 days after signing of this order, and one revision will be made after corrections to draft by Rosalyn Williams. Final copy due not later than 90 days following signing of this order.

TERMS: $1,250 will be paid to Mr. Horner on delivery of the draft. A remaining $1,425 will be paid to Mr. Horner on acceptance of final camera-ready copy.

Please sign and return one copy of this order.

_____   _____
Signed by Gerry Williams   Signed by Henry Horner

business. That is why one can, and often does, simply use a letterhead to draft the occasional purchase order it needs.

If you are required to sign and return one copy of the purchase order, the signed copy acts as a contract because all five conditions are met, presumably. The offer and consideration are stipulated, your signature signifies acceptance, and it is a premise that you and your client are both of legal age and legally competent to enter into a contract. Purchase orders, both formal and informal ones, are thus used frequently to contract for small projects.

> Purchase orders that meet the five conditions are simple contracts and fully enforceable.

Letter of Agreement

A letter of agreement (See Figure 10.2) is another simple way to enter into a written contract for a small project, and is quite similar to that informal purchase order. The letter may originate with either party, describe the work and the consideration, and provide a place to sign acceptance by each party. Again, it is presumed that the parties are of age and legally competent so that the letter is a legal contract.

> Letters of agreement that meet the five conditions are simple contracts and fully enforceable.

These informal documents are not suitable to contract for major projects because they lack the clauses that are normally included in contracts for large projects, clauses that are written to stipulate certain requirements and conditions and to anticipate future questions that may arise. The clauses thus are designed to minimize disputes and other problems that could arise out of questions not anticipated but answered in advance.

FIGURE 10.2   A typical letter of agreement.

Gerry Williams & Co.
Investments
Whitestone Building, Suite 917
San Diego, CA 71989

January 10, 2000

Mr. Henry Horner
P.O. Box 17863
Los Angeles, CA 90123

Dear Mr. Horner:

The following is a statement of a service you have agreed to provide to this company, along with relevant other details of our verbal agreement, which this letter documents:

Development of a 6 x 9 brochure and sales letter for a direct mail sales campaign announcing the opening of the Gerry Williams Investment Services. First draft of each item will be delivered not later than 45 days after signing of this letter, and one revision will be made after corrections to draft by Rosalyn Williams. Final copy due not later than 90 days following signing of this letter.

$1,250 will be paid to you on delivery of the draft. A remaining $1,425 will be paid to you on acceptance of final camera-ready copy.

Please sign and return one copy of this letter.

_____   _____
Signed by Gerry Williams   Signed by Henry Horner

CONTRACTS MAY BE DECLARED INVALID

Because those five conditions are mandatory, it is possible to have a contract declared invalid when a judge or jury is convinced that the contract is invalid because one of the parties to the contract was not of legal age, was otherwise not competent to enter into a contract, had been coerced or forced to sign the contract, or had been deliberately deceived and thus unfairly lured into signing; or the contract was for an illegal activity. It is a general truth that once you sign on the dotted line you can't get out of what you agreed to, but there are exceptions to the general truth, and court battles are fought every day because of those exceptions.

FORMAL CONTRACTS

Obviously, it is best to have a formal contract written and not rely on memory or the parties' honesty to ensure that the terms of the contract are met. Otherwise, when disputes arise about what was agreed to, as they often do, it becomes most difficult to settle. That often results in a costly legal battle in court, where judge and jury try to determine what the original agreement was and what is equitable. Even the most carefully drawn contract can be challenged, and many are.

A contract can be documented by a simple statement or two scrawled on a brown paper bag. If you watch any of the several court or judge shows on daytime television today, you will see many such informal contracts scrawled on notepaper, the back of a menu, a napkin, or other highly informal medium, and you will see the judges scrutinizing these contracts closely because they are the best available indicators of what the parties agreed to originally. Such a contract is often only slightly more effective than a verbal contract, for there is much more to the typical contract than the five obligatory factors. Here is what you may expect to find included in most formally drawn up contracts:

✔ An introductory statement identifying the parties to the contract.

✔ Stipulation of the offer and acceptance.

✔ Description of the work to be done.

✔ Stipulation of the consideration.

✔ A number of clauses.

✔ Signatures of the agreeing parties and of witnesses.

CLAUSES

Formal contracts normally include more than one agreement. There is, of course, the basic agreement for the services to be provided and payment for them, but in a full-blown, formal contract there are a number of other agreements included as *clauses*. Some of them are agreements protecting some interest of one or the other party, while other clauses are agreements that are designed to avoid disputes or, at least, to provide a means to settle disputes that arise.

You will encounter, in contracts for your services, many clauses that will become familiar to you because they are standard clauses, even if the language used in them varies a little from one contract to another. There are a great many standard clauses and an almost unlimited number that may be written especially for the contract. Following are a few—only a few—of the most common clauses you will find used in contracts for your services:

✔ *Confidentiality*. This is a clause in which you agree to hold in strictest confidence that information you learn on the job which is, to the client, proprietary and *confidential*. It may be information pertaining to the client's finances, processes, marketing, or other matters, but it is information that the client does not wish to have known outside his or her own walls. As an experienced pro-

clauses
sections of a contract that are supplementary agreements on peripheral, but important, interests of one party or the other.

confidential
characteristic of information that one holds to be private property.

fessional, you will usually perceive without being told that certain information being made known to you is of a confidential nature and is to be held in that confidence. Your opinion of the information does not have any bearing. That is, information that the client holds to be confidential may be, in your opinion, ancient and obsolete data that is of no value to anyone. However, that opinion does not relieve you of the obligation to treat that information as confidential once you know that the client so regards it.

✔ *Noncompete.* This is a clause in contracts under which you are employed by a broker and assigned to work for the broker's client. You agree here not to accept direct employment or an independent contract with the broker's client for some period of time, such as six months or a year, following your assignment. Some clauses of this type provide that you may accept employment with the client if the client pays the broker a fee. (The broker has usually signed a separate agreement with the client to cover this, if such is the case.) Be sure to read noncompete clauses carefully. Some try to set unreasonable lengths of time, such as five years during which you may not accept employment or contracts with the broker's client.

✔ *Compensation.* This describes what, when, and how you will be paid, and may include penalties for late payment. This is a clause that merits close scrutiny before you accept it.

✔ *Disputes.* This stipulates measures, such as *arbitration*, for handling disputes.

✔ *Governing law.* Needed when your client is in another state or the work is to be done in another state than the one in which you have your office, this specifies agreement on which state's law will govern settlement of any dispute (because state laws do vary in many important details).

arbitration
method of resolving disputes through the services of a third party, outside the courts and law, accepted by the disputants to help find a basis for settling.

✔ *Assignment.* Any asset may be assigned to another party, but the most common use of an *assignment* clause is to make clear an agreement that you may assign your receivables to another party. Usually, this is used to discount (sell) your receivables to a bank or factor, and so convert your asset into ready cash.

assignment
transferring title of an asset, such as a receivable, to another party for a consideration.

Most contracts include a number of clauses, which are themselves agreements on specific points that might otherwise lead to serious disputes.

DEFINING WHAT IS TO BE DONE

The contract must include some definition or description of what is to be done under the contract. That may be some simple action that can be adequately described in a paragraph or two. However, many contracts are for complex projects that require many months to complete and are described adequately only by a complete set of specifications. In such cases, it is often the practice to include that description by reference or attachment to the contract. That set of specifications is thus a document attached to the contract as an appended exhibit or a proposal named by the contract and thus included in the contract by reference. This is another example of the importance of having a proposal and of preparing it with great care: It may become the heart of the contract. It is because of this that a client will want a proposal formally amended and updated to reflect any agreements reached that mean changes agreed to since the proposal was written. You, too, should want to document those changes by amending your proposal, since your proposal will be a key part of the contract.

> The portion of your proposal that specifies the work, the end items to be delivered, and other such details will eventually be part of the contract; hence its importance.

NEGOTIATION

Contracts, even the most informal and simplest ones, are negotiated, even if you do not realize that your discussion is a negotiation. Asking a shopkeeper to provide an item from his or her shelves, having a price named, and agreeing (or refusing to agree) to it is a simple negotiation. Usually, when a simple contract instrument such as a purchase order or letter of agreement is signed, the negotiation has been completed beforehand, and the execution of the written document is routine. However, it is sometimes the case that one of the parties offers a letter of agreement (that may originate with either party) or the client issues a purchase order without a clear understanding in advance, and some negotiation must then take place before the signing. That is not likely to be a very extended or lengthy negotiation in the case of such a small project, and may very well be conducted by telephone and any agreements implemented by initialed pen-and-ink changes to the document. Even with government agencies, it may be and often is as simple and informal as having the client call to have you verify your price, schedule, and readiness to begin work.

For larger projects, the two parties sit down at a table with whatever relevant documents are at hand—a proposal or a draft contract on paper—and discuss their wants and needs, bargaining with each other and trying to reach compromises and/or trades to achieve an agreement. Such negotiations can involve entire teams of negotiators from each side. (We were five negotiators on each side of the table, struggling for two days to reach agreement on a set of contract terms for a multimillion-dollar Job Corps contract.)

Negotiating Philosophies

Where you find yourself doing business regularly with a client, you learn the client's likes, dislikes, and bargaining style, and he or she learns yours. Soon, you may find that negotiations go smoothly with that client because of that mutual understanding. Some negotiators believe firmly in *win-lose negotiating*, and will always try to be the winner and make you the loser, not necessarily out of greed or even aggressiveness, but because they enjoy negotiating—jousting even—as an I win, you lose contest.

There is another negotiating philosophy, the win-win school. In *win-win negotiating*, the object is to find for every sticking point a compromise with which both parties are satisfied and neither feels coerced or bullied into accepting the other's position. The philosophy is that it is not a good contract if either party is not truly satisfied with the outcome of the negotiation.

Assuming that you know nothing about the negotiating style of the client, you need to try to assess it. If your client plays hardball at the negotiating table, win-lose negotiating, you are quite likely to be the underdog in the exchange. Normally, the client has the advantage in this kind of negotiation because you want the contract and have invested time and money in an effort to win it. The client, presumably, has other bidders ready to deal, or so you surmise, so you are treading cautiously. You can try to use win-lose tactics here, but you probably stand a better chance of winning the contract with win-win negotiating tactics, trying to reach agreements through reasonable compromises or even with some inventive ideas.

win-lose negotiating
negotiating to try to win everything possible.

win-win negotiating
negotiating to try to reach compromises on all disputes that will satisfy both parties that they reached a fair exchange.

Negotiation is win-lose or win-win. You need to decide which is the kind your client uses if you are to have a fair chance of winning an acceptable contract.

Chapter

11

Client Relationships and Ethical Considerations

Client relationships and ethical considerations in conducting an independent consulting practice are often closely related.

IDENTIFYING YOUR CLIENT

When you are retained by a very small business, you generally deal face-to-face with the proprietor, so there is no doubt in your mind as to who is your client. When you deal with a larger organization, especially a corporation, knowing who your client is may be much less clear. That is, in doing business with a large corporation, which of the following should you regard as your client? (There may be other candidates for recognition as your client, but these are the most likely ones.)

- ✔ The chief executive officer (CEO) of the corporation.
- ✔ The staff member with whom you negotiated for your services.
- ✔ The executive who signed your contract.

✔ The corporate project manager or sales manager with whom you interface in providing your services and who must approve your work.

✔ Some other individual.

Uncertainty in deciding who is your client may lead to ethical problems, conflicting instructions, conflicts in working relationships, and/or other difficulties that can affect your reputation and your contract, and even to your doing a great deal of extra work for which you will never be paid. It is necessary, therefore, to be clear on this question and to get orders from only a proper representative of the organization. However, determining who that is may not be always as simple as it may appear.

> When a large organization retains you, your client is whoever has the authority to represent the organization. But how can you be sure who that is?

Normally, you operate on the reasonable premise that whoever pays your fee is your client, and it is the corporation that pays your fee. That individual who represents the corporation with regard to your assignment is thus your client for practical purposes. That seems to be a logical assumption, but perhaps it is not a sound idea in all cases, such as the following:

Many years ago, I was retained by IBM to write a manual on a large U.S. Air Force communications system. The first day I arrived on the job at IBM, I was greeted by the executive who had interviewed and hired me. (I will call him Ben here.) Ben now introduced me to a lower-level supervisor who was to be my immediate interface with IBM for the project. I was presented with some *boilerplate* instructions concerning the project and asked by the latter to prepare a working outline of the manual I proposed to begin writing.

boilerplate
standard copy, as language for a clause used commonly.

I prepared an outline based on my original understanding of the requirement, per my original discussions with Ben. The supervisor immediately objected to the outline, saying that my approach was all wrong. I thought it was his approach that was all wrong and not at all in line with my original understanding of what I was to write. However, faced with dogmatic insistence from this supervisor that he knew better, and unwilling to make an issue of the matter on my first day or make a formal complaint to Ben, I gave in and revised the outline.

A day later, Ben asked me to come to his office, where he expressed his total disappointment with my outline. I handed him a copy of my original outline. Ben read it, nodding his head slightly in what seemed to be approval, and then asked for an explanation.

After Ben heard me out, he said something to me I shall never forget: "I retained you because you appeared to me to be the true professional I needed to write the introductory manual on the system. How could you compromise your integrity and agree to do something you knew was all wrong?"

A TWOFOLD OBLIGATION

Of course, Ben was right and completely justified in what he said. I recognized that immediately, and I was deeply humiliated at my own professional lapse, which was, of course, shameful. I had permitted this supervisor to become my client and dictate to me action I was sure was not what my true client, IBM (represented by Ben), wanted, and for which I had been selected as the specialist who would do the job. I knew that this lower-level supervisor was not representing IBM fairly because he had taken it upon himself to settle our dispute by implying that I would be sent on my way if I continued to resist making the changes he dictated. To yield to him and allow him to become my client, when I was sure that he was wrong, was failing to protect my true client's interests, as I was morally obligated to do. That is a most important distinction to make when faced with a situation of this kind, and it is why you need to know your true client and understand your mission. In fact, your obligation is a double one: It is implicit in your contract that you are obliged to protect your client's interests in regard to the work you are doing, but you also have a moral obligation to yourself to do the right thing and protect your own reputation.

> You have an obligation to understand and protect your client's interests as they relate to the work for which you were retained, and you have a personal reputation to protect.

Your client is, indeed, whoever has retained you and is paying you, although your client may be represented by some individual who speaks for the client. (For convenience, we will refer to that individual as the client's project manager or PM.) Presumably, you have a clear idea what you are to do for your client, as expressed in a purchase order, contract, or letter of agreement. You therefore know or should know whether the PM is truly representing your client with respect to your assignment or perhaps representing himself or herself through being mistaken or due to a less noble cause. Depending on that assessment of yours, you may or may not regard the PM as your client and qualified as such to approve, disapprove, or otherwise influence the work you are doing for your client.

I have also encountered variants of this situation, in which subordinates happen to disagree with their superiors' view of a program and try to make an end play to change things, usually in a way that enables them to blame you if things go wrong for them. Such was the case when I sent a writer to gather information for a proposal we had been invited to write and submit. My writer visited an individual named in the client's RFP as the contact person who would answer questions. This individual disagreed violently with the organization's proposed program and what had been written in the original RFP to describe the client's requirement. He led my writer completely astray, as we discovered later when we were debriefed and asked how we had gotten so far off the track. If you accept this kind of spokesperson as your client—as someone speaking for and reflecting the desires of the organization—you will be gathering false information and being made a victim. This does not happen often, fortunately, but it does happen. Again, when you run into a contradiction such as this, you must ask yourself whether this individual is or speaks for the client and act accordingly to protect your client first, and yourself second.

Ordinarily and in most cases, you will have no trouble treating your client's PM or other spokesperson as the client. But that is based on an assumption that the person is honest, knows what he or she is doing, and imparts to you directives or guidance that is compatible with what you were retained to do. If any of these assumptions is wrong, you are faced with a serious dilemma: how to proceed. If this is a situation where you are preparing to submit a proposal or make a presentation of some other kind, you will have to seek out a more authoritative source and get the correct information.

VERBAL REQUEST FOR ADDITIONAL WORK

A usually effective reaction to any problem such as those described here is to require any new information that contradicts or veers sharply from the information you were given when you started to be in writing. Let us consider the not uncommon problem of dealing with a client's project manager who is trying to pressure you into making changes or doing additional work on your project without offering you authorization, such as an *engineering change notice (ECN)* or other paper that commits your client.

engineering change notice (ECN)
a form used by most engineering offices to document a change.

"Don't worry about it," you are smugly assured. "You'll get paid for it. You'll get the paperwork later."

But "later" may never arrive, and your claim falls on deaf ears. The individual who persuaded you to carry out unauthorized changes is not to be found, has left the company, or "can't remember" the whole thing.

Handling the Problem

The first step is to ask for a letter or memorandum authorizing the requested changes and agreeing to appropriate changes in your compensation. If that is not forthcoming, have a serious discussion with the PM and make it as clear as you can that you cannot and will not depart from what you originally agreed to do, unless there is a *contract amendment* or paperwork committing the client to the change in the work originally contracted. Such changes in a project are common enough, but it is risky to agree to make them on the basis of a verbal authorization, especially one from an employee who is not at a high enough level to commit the company. Requiring an amendment or letter documenting a client-dictated change to the contract is your protection and assures you that management at the proper level—the contract-signing level—approves the changes. It does require a great deal of tact to do this without offending the individual, of course. You must be very careful that the PM does not interpret your request as questioning the PM's honesty or competence. Usually, a rather casually stated requirement for a contract amendment, with a smiling, "Just business, you know," will be inoffensive. (I have never had much difficulty doing such things as this in a thoroughly businesslike way by doing them quietly as a completely routine matter of no special significance.)

contract amendment changes in contract, usually written, agreed to by both parties.

> Do not accept changes to your contract based on verbal requests or assurances. They must be in writing, signed by an official who can commit the organization to changes.

Doing the right thing protects your reputation and image, but it also protects your client, as it should. Protecting your client's interests should be an important ethical requirement. In doing work under large contracts, I have been congratulated and thanked by senior executives for refusing to accept changes by verbal orders.

It Happens in Government Work, Too

In dealing with the government as a client, a different kind of situation may arise, one that can be confusing. In some government contracts, a number of people may have to "sign off on the project"—sign approval of what was done or delivered. It was my fate once to be under contract to the Federal Aviation Administration (FAA) to prepare a report on what progress the FAA had made in its safety programs in the current fiscal year. The department included approximately 20 engineers, all of whom would review my draft and comment. Not too surprisingly, some approved my draft and signed off, some made minor changes and signed off, and some refused to sign off. Ultimately, as the project went far beyond its scheduled date while trying to get 100 percent approval by the staff and the engineers still argued, the contracting officer called me and said that he despaired of ever getting that staff of engineers to reach agreement, so he wanted to cancel the remainder of the contract. However, he wished to avoid the difficult legal procedure of novation, and he asked for any ideas I could offer. I did know a much simpler way to cancel further work on that contract and end it without novation, and together we worked out the details so that we were both satisfied. I had no hesitancy about this because the contracting officer certainly spoke for the agency, and we were going to do all the proper paperwork so all would be entirely legal. I believed that I was doing the right thing for my client, so I was perfectly willing to satisfy the client in any way I could do so ethically and legally.

HOW FRIENDLY SHOULD YOU BE?

As an independent consultant, I have sometimes worked shoulder to shoulder with my client's employees in a bull pen office area, sometimes had a private office on the client's premises, sometimes worked entirely in my own office on my own premises, and sometimes had some combination of these working arrangements. You may expect to encounter and work under any of these conditions, although there are hazards in a long-term arrangement working on the client's premises: Regular staff employees tend often to be somewhat suspicious and resentful of consultants, whom they regard as interlopers on their turf and potential hazards to their own positions. Or, if you are a naturally gregarious individual, you may become much too well acquainted with the client's regular employees, and therefore too friendly with them. That is usually a mistake for any of these reasons:

- ✔ It may appear to the client that you are spending (or wasting) too much time with the staff employees and neglecting your own obligations.
- ✔ You run the risk of inadvertently offending one or more of the client's staff, who may then retaliate in some manner.
- ✔ You may be propelled into the awkward situation of being invited to lunch, picnics, or other social activities and being forced to find a way to decline diplomatically and risk giving offense.

Here are a few do and don't suggestions that should help you avoid the worst of these hazards:

- ✔ Do not allow yourself to be drawn into an office clique, or even be a listener lurking on its fringes.
- ✔ Resist, diplomatically, questions from the staff about how you became a consultant, how others can do so, how much more a consultant earns,

who you know in the company, how you manage to get yourself retained, and other such inquiries.

✔ Keep in mind that the right course is to be friendly, even amiable, but don't go far beyond greetings and smiles of recognition. Be conscious that you are not one of them and be careful that you do not appear to be trying to become one of them.

A TYPICAL CASE

In many consulting assignments, it will be necessary to talk at length with many of the client's staff, and even to maintain an ongoing relationship with them for the duration of your contract. You will try to be friendly without getting chummy, while maintaining a businesslike exterior. But there are often some thin-skinned individuals, especially in cases where your very presence as a consultant and outsider makes staff people apprehensive and perhaps resentful. Some will be offended to some degree, no matter how inoffensive you try to be, and you may have the bad luck to be dealing with one of these. In practice, I have found that even when that is the case, if you are patient and maintain an air of objectivity, those individuals eventually overcome their umbrage and accept the situation. That some individuals will get offended is unfortunate, of course, but you must not let that prevent you from always doing the right thing to protect your own interests and those of your client. Here is an example:

On one occasion, before the desktop computer era, I was one of a team retained by a prominent computer manufacturer that had built a computer for the government—for a military agency, it so happens. The computer was a success, but the manuals were rejected by the agency. The company had no experience in writing military manuals, which are admittedly of a special nature, and so we were brought in as experienced technical writers to rewrite the manuals the company's staff of writers had written. Early in the project, I approached the lead writer of the company's publications staff and asked a few technical questions about the computer. I sensed very quickly that the writer was most uncomfortable in the technical area, when he gave me rather evasive answers to my technical questions. I then asked what I thought was an innocent and inoffensive question—to whom I ought to talk in order to get some technical information about the computer.

He was immediately offended and on the defensive at what he interpreted as my attack on his professional competence. It was not an attack; I did not expect him to be an engineer but felt it was a necessary courtesy to ask him the questions I did before taking my research elsewhere. I withdrew as discreetly as I could and took up my research in the engineering department, seeking out the engineering staff members who could help me.

> You can't always know who will be thin-skinned and take offense at even innocent actions. It is a good idea to assume that everyone is that sensitive, at least until you know better.

Ultimately, about three months later, having reviewed my draft manuscript as required by his company, he approved the draft and came to my desk to congratulate me on it and apologize for his earlier surliness. We then developed an excellent working relationship, during which we conferred on many matters with which we were both concerned. (Incidentally, this was also one of the cases where the company management offered me a staff job if I would agree to stay on!)

SPECIAL ETHICAL CONSIDERATIONS

We judge those with whom we do business by their *professional ethics* in general, including the guarantees they offer, their readiness to make good on their guarantees, their honesty overall, and many other factors in connection with how most of us believe business owners should behave. And, regardless of whether we are conscious of it, we are greatly influenced by their friendliness and courtesy. As business owners, we should be always conscious of how our clients and prospective clients view us in this respect.

professional ethics
a code of proper behavior and standards for independent consultants.

Conflicts of Interest

Many of the ethical considerations of which we must be conscious involve *conflicts of interest*. Usually, the conflict is between the client's interest and our own personal interest. For example, you may find an opportunity to charge a client for work you planned to do, but later found was unnecessary. Therefore, your costs were well below your estimate. Should you count yourself fortunate or adjust your bill in the client's favor? Probably that depends on the provisions of your original contract, on whether you offered to do the job for a flat, fixed price or on some hourly or daily fee basis, such as a *time and material contract*. You must decide what is the right thing to do. (That may vary from one case to another, and so require individual assessment of all factors each time.)

On the other hand, some conflicts of interest and views of what are the right things to do are much clearer. You clearly should not use one client's proprietary information to benefit another client, to win another client's business, or for any purpose other than in the interest of the client to whom the information belongs.

Sometimes, even when there is not a conflict of interest it may appear that such a conflict exists, and that is as bad as if it really did. (Once again, we must be con-

conflict of interest
having an interest that is in opposition to your obligation to your client and may therefore color your judgment and make it difficult or you to be objective and ethical.

time and material contract
a contract in which one is paid for his or her time at an agreed-upon rate and reimbursed for all materials used.

cerned with the client's perception of truth.) If you must prove that there is no such conflict, the damage is done, and you will never again appear to that client to be totally trustworthy. There will forever be a lingering sour taste in connection with you.

> Beware even the mere appearance of an ethical offense of any kind. It can be almost as deadly in its effects as an actual ethical misstep. You must try to be purer than Caesar's wife.

Professional Behavior

As an independent consultant, you are a professional person and should always be mindful of that.

- ✔ You are not a huckster, and should not make extravagant promises and use a great deal of hyperbole, either in writing or in speech.
- ✔ Raising your visibility means making yourself better known as a consultant specialist, not as a bon vivant, omnipresent backslapper, or generally outspoken boor.
- ✔ Focus on facts, not claims, when marketing your services.
- ✔ Never market your services while on billable time, especially not when you are on a client's premises. (There are a few consultants whose first act, when arriving on a client's premises, is to get on the client's telephone and call everyone to leave the number where they can be reached during the day.)
- ✔ Never criticize, condemn, or sneer at your competitors, neither in general nor by individual names.

✔ Be mindful of your personal dignity, and conduct yourself accordingly. If, in making a presentation of any kind, you wish to use humor, be sure it is not coarse humor. Avoid the hazards of making minorities, handicapped people, and/or other identifiable groups the butt of your humor. Whatever that group, there is almost certainly someone in earshot who will be offended and perhaps even outraged. (At the very least, you will have demonstrated bad taste.) The only safe butt for your humor is yourself. As far as I know, I have never offended anyone by telling tales of foolish mistakes I made.

✔ When you sell your services by hours or days or when you are required to report these, be scrupulously honest in your accounts. Some clients will believe that you are padding your accounts no matter how honest you are, but your conscience will be clear. (I almost always put in more hours than the number for which I bill clients.)

✔ Be truthful, while tactful, in conversations and correspondence with clients and vendors.

✔ Deliver everything you promise to the very best of your ability.

A Very Special Ethical Requirement

As consultants, we have a few special ethical obligations because our work often makes us privy to our clients' proprietary and confidential information, very much as physicians and lawyers are. We must therefore be conscientious in safeguarding each client's confidentiality. (See Chapter 10.) It is an especially important matter, one that merits stress in discussing it, and so it is mentioned more than once in these pages.

The most obvious hazard is that of carelessness, of revealing confidential and proprietary information in casual conversation, but a worse hazard is that we may, consciously or unconsciously, use such information to help us gain other contracts by agreeing to use it to help a new client in some way. Not only is this a violation of the prime reason that clients ask you to sign confidentiality agreements, but it tells the new client that you are not to be trusted with confidential information. (If you can't be trusted with a former client's information, why should the new client trust you with his or her information?)

As a general rule, avoid discussing any of your clients, former clients, or even former projects. It can sometimes be difficult to judge what should be regarded as proprietary information for at least two reasons: One, you may not always be sure if something you know originated as confidential information gained while helping another client; and, two, you may not be sure if something you learned while working for another client was truly confidential information or common knowledge. Thus, it is not always easy to respect and keep confidentiality agreements. You must work at it.

Many of these matters, such as that of safeguarding the client's confidentiality, are covered in agreements you signed in accepting the assignment. Many contracts are boilerplated in advance with clauses covering such matters. Be sure to read your contract carefully; it will define much of the ethical code you should respect and follow. (See Chapter 10 for brief discussions of several of these clauses and the matters they cover.)

Chapter

Some Commonsense Notes about Writing

Grammar and other rules of usage are only a part, a relatively small part and, in some respects, one of the less important considerations in writing well.

WHY A CHAPTER ON WRITING

The ability to write well is a great asset to everyone, and is especially valuable to an independent sales consultant. Besides the importance of writing skills with their many applications to creating and managing ancillary consulting services such as writing and speaking (see Chapter 9), there is also the fact that all sales activities involve written materials to a large extent. Depending on the services you choose to provide to clients, you may spend a good bit of your time creating copy for written products you produce and for presentations you make from the speaker's platform. It is something of an inconvenience to be forced to rely on other specialists for help with writing and related editorial chores. Conversely, it gives you a great advantage if you can do all or most of these things yourself. Or, even if you prefer to hire others to handle writing tasks for you, having good writing skills of your own confers on you an ability to judge the suitability of material written by others and do a bit of editing, which is in itself a most useful consulting skill.

> As a sales consultant, you will find more than one use for writing skills of your own.

Despite a good deal of popular belief to the contrary, writing skill is not a genetic inheritance, something you (or anyone else) does naturally. It is a learned ability, even if the learning is acquired unconsciously, as it is by many who may appear to be born writers because they have no difficulty expressing themselves in writing. As with most things, there are lots of myths and mistaken ideas about writing, propagated out of ignorance to some degree, but also repeated with enthusiasm as rationalizations by those who do not write well and feel a need to account for their inability to express themselves effectively in writing.

There is, of course, no need for such rationalizations: It is not that difficult to develop competence in writing proper prose. (One need not be a great writer to be a thoroughly competent one.) In this chapter, we are going to look at writing from some commonsense viewpoints and try to take some of the mystery out of writing well. We will avoid, as much as possible, any classroom-type discussions of writing. Even where we must touch on some technical points, we will refrain from the jargon of grammarians and try to explain each point in everyday commonsense terms. For starters, here are a few truths on the subject that may surprise you:

- ✔ Hardly anyone writes a good first draft. Professional writers know that, and they accept the premise that they will have to rewrite, revise, and polish everything they write before it is ready to print or be published.

✔ Epigram resulting from the preceding point: All good writing is rewriting. Virtually everything you read in published form has been edited and rewritten not only once, but several times in most cases. Rewriting includes self-editing. If you are able to do a good job of editing your own first draft, you can feel free to write as much as you want in that first draft, and clean it up by self-editing and revising it. Writing everything freely in your draft because you know that you will edit and revise it is what leads to good copy.

✔ Some writers are known for elegance: Henry James was, for example. But some excellent writers have a very simple style. Ernest Hemingway was a master of that style. He wasn't born with the talent to write that way. At an early point in his career, while working on a newspaper, his editor drummed simplicity ("just the facts") into his head. Even much of Shakespeare's most insightful and most often quoted writings were expressed by him in simple direct thoughts, using various stops as punctuation. You can never go wrong with that style.

✔ Your readers will not normally be interested in your style, in any case. (We are not talking about creating literature or works of great entertainment here.) They are interested in what you have to tell them, the facts, presented in an easily understandable way.

✔ No one is a born writer (that was stated earlier, but it merits repeating), although skillful writing may come more easily to one person than it does to another. That is mostly because some people truly enjoy writing and practice it a great deal. Practice is a key to skill: The more you write, the easier writing becomes for you. Voracious reading also appears to be a great help in learning to write easily and fluently.

A modern myth that seems to be gaining some currency, especially among those who spend a great deal of their time at computer keyboards and exploring cyberspace, is this: Writing and publishing are less and less used today, with computers, satellites, TV, and other modern developments making them less needed. That is, of course, most untrue. Visit any large newsstand and witness the vast array of periodicals that come off the presses every day. Look at the shelves of a modern bookstore, and see many of the 50,000 to 60,000 new books published each year, supplementing the millions of books remaining on the shelves from previous years.

Even in cyberspace itself, consider the facts: E-mail is by far the most used facility of computers in cyberspace, and many of the millions of computer owners use their computers primarily for e-mail. (As e-mail has become more and more popular, I find my fax machine gathering dust.) Consider also the thousands of newsgroups that are present in cyberspace entirely as words appearing on screens, and the words that dominate the web sites and other presentations on your computer screen. The forms of presentation are evolving and changing to some small degree, and we may be using less paper to communicate our words (although even that seems doubtful), but we are writing more words than ever, as millions who would rarely write a conventional letter write billions of words of e-mail and other methods of expression for presentation on PC screens every day.

> You need to write more, rather than less, today, with the demands of e-mail and other developments of the cyberspace age.

MOST OF US ALREADY HAVE THE BASICS

We all receive a basic education on the use of our language, American English. That education stresses courses in the mechanics of usage—spelling, grammar, punctuation, and other rules. (In the modern view, most of these are really guidelines, rather than rules.) We also undergo relevant literature appreciation courses, with required reading of certain approved books, and we are made to practice writing skills by writing essays, book reports, letters, and other such homework. Most of us thus learn to communicate in writing, at least well enough for the practical requirements of everyday private life and working life.

> You already know how to write, but if you are one of the many who avoid writing as much as possible, you need to learn how to write well.

For some reason, the study of English appears to be one of the least liked courses among students, especially that portion that deals with learning the rules. That latter fact considered, it is perhaps not at all surprising that relatively few adults truly like to write, and many, if not most, do everything they can to avoid it.

One way I have especially noted this truth is the reaction I get when I write a vendor for information or for other help in using the vendor's product. (I am one of that apparently small minority who prefer to express oneself in writing, rather than in telephone conversation.) It takes forever to get a response when I write such an inquiry, and then it is often made obvious to me that if I want a prompt response I must call, not write. I infer from this that a great many people find that talking is easy, and writing is difficult.

I would express the difference between talking and writing this way: You can simply rattle on interminably in conversation, but writing requires that you *think*. You must think out what you want to say and find the words that you believe will get your point across. Thinking is hard work, so a great many people seek ways to avoid that strenuous effort by what appears to be the easy alternative: conversation.

Of course, I am biased in this matter. I am biased by the fact that I am a professional writer, editor, and publications manager of many years' experience, and also by the fact that I am one of those odd individuals who actually *like* to write. In managing writers and helping them learn to write better, if not write well, I soon learned that the principal reason so many did not write very well had little or nothing to do with how well they had learned and remembered the mechanics of usage—the grammar, spelling, and punctuation. It had a great deal more to do with their more directly related mental processes: how well they knew and understood the subject they were writing about, and how clearly they had established in their minds both who their reader was and what they wished to have the reader understand as a result of reading what they were writing. (In writing, you must remember that your writing is intended to convey certain knowledge to the reader and to enable the reader to do something.)

> How well you write is largely a result of how well you understand the subject about which you are writing, your reader, and what main point(s) you wish to make about the subject.

Recently, in an Internet forum on writing, one author of computer books stated that it is easy to write a how-to book. One needs only to gather the information, edit it, and present it, he said. I could not help but respond and point out that there are also the not inconsiderable chores of analyzing, interpreting, and organizing the information and its presentation, not to mention making suggestions and recommendations for its use, if the book is to be truly a how-to book. Too, I thought the writer passed much too lightly over the matter of research, which he dismissed as "gathering the information," which he apparently regards as a routine chore of no great importance. In fact, one exceptionally successful writer, James Michener, revealed that he devoted as much as two years to research before beginning to write a new book. Great research, versus casual research, can be the difference between a great book and a mediocre potboiler.

In any case, we will not discuss here the academic subjects of grammar, punctuation, and other such elements of writing. If you happen to feel a need to refresh yourself in these matters, a trip to a nearby bookstore or public library will put you in touch with many relevant texts you can use for that purpose, or you can find many computer programs to teach the subject and others that will analyze what you write and offer corrections. Here, we will assume that you know enough of the basics so that there is little need of discussing these and other elements of writing; they will be mentioned only as absolutely necessary, and even then in as practical and nontechnical a way as possible.

WRITING "WHAT YOU KNOW"

A piece of advice often offered to aspirants to writing is, "Write only about what you know." That is too often taken by the aspirants to mean write only about whatever you already know, what you happen to have learned so far in your life and believe you know quite well. There is an underlying validity in this admonition to write about what you know, but there are at least two things wrong with that injunction also. They are wrong because they are not precisely spelled out. "What you know" is far too vague, because "know" is far too vague. You need to understand, rather than know. You must understand the subject well enough to qualify as an expert of at least a junior grade so that what you write on the subject is in adequate detail to satisfy the objective of your writing and is entirely accurate.

The other weakness in the admonition is the implication that you may write only about that in which you are already highly knowledgeable. That implication ignores the truth that you need not limit yourself by choosing to write about a subject in which you are already an expert. Most professional writers are not experts in the subject when they decide to write about it. Instead, they undertake the necessary research to become expert in the subject. In my own case, I wrote more than one successful book on contracting with the government because my direct experience in doing so had made me expert in the subject, so I needed to do very little original research. But when I undertook to write what became a successful book on contracts and negotiations, I depended to only a small degree on my personal knowledge and experience, relying primarily and much more heavily on many hours of extensive research in four very large university-level textbooks on contract law, each written by a team of law professors. The more I researched the subject, the more I understood it, and the more I understood the subject, the more easily the words flowed from my fingers poised on the keyboard. (By using four textbooks in my research, whatever was not completely clear to me in one text was clearer in another, so the use of multiple sources was clearly a great advantage and is the way good researchers check out the facts they are researching and their understanding of the material—i.e., from other sources.)

Try that for yourself. Try to write a short essay on any subject you think you know pretty well. Then lay it aside and do some research on the subject. Research it until you think you are really quite knowledgeable about that subject. Then try writing that little essay again. You will be surprised at how easy it is. And then reread your original effort and learn what an enormous difference your research has made in your writing ability as well as in your knowledge. It is likely to be one of the most valuable lessons of your life. It alone can transform your writing ability. You will become aware of how important it is to be totally honest with yourself on how much you know about a given subject. In at least some cases, reluctance to write is a result of the individual knowing on some level, probably not fully consciously, that he or she does not know enough about the subject, so research cures that ill. It helps you to be more honest with yourself and gain some insight into your own drives and impulses.

HOW MUCH RESEARCH?

To select from a dozen oranges the largest, ripest, firmest, and juiciest, you must examine the entire dozen. Likewise, with research: You can choose the best or most appropriate information on the subject only by gathering and examining—researching—all the information. Characteristically in writing you use only a portion of the information you have searched out, probably as little as one-third or perhaps even less than that. That does not mean that you researched more than was necessary. Quite the contrary, you had to look at all the information to evaluate what was important information and what was trivia, and what your reader will need to know and what is unnecessary data. Research enables you to choose the material you need. What is left is residue, to be discarded or, perhaps, to be stored away for possible reference.

But how do you decide which portions of the information are suitable for your purposes and which are not? That brings up an activity that would have occurred before the research: planning. The more thoroughly you plan what you intend to write, the easier it is to carry out all the other major functions of writing. Here are the key steps of the entire process:

- ✔ Research.
- ✔ Sifting and sorting the research data.
- ✔ Organizing the selected material.
- ✔ Outlining.
- ✔ Writing.
- ✔ Review and rewriting.

> In carrying out research, you have specific aims to select information that is suitable for your writing needs, and you should have these in mind as you carry out the research.

IN THE BEGINNING

You may start your writing project with any of several intentions or assumptions. In most cases, probably, you start out with the intention of making some major point or argument, as I did when I set out to explain how any small business, even that of an independent entrepreneur, could seek and win government contracts. That objective automatically included a definition of my intended reader (a small business owner or entrepreneur) and helped me decide on a preliminary—quite rough and general—outline. Later, when I had collected enough information from my research (largely done from my own experience, in this case). I would develop and refine my outline to furnish a somewhat detailed guide for my writing.

Although I outline mentally when preparing to write something brief, it's a good idea to write your outline for even a small piece of writing. The act of outlining on paper compels you to think out your presentation in advance, while it also helps you to do so. However, your outlines are not etched in stone, and may be modified, as necessary, even after you are deeply into the writing. Try to remain flexible, regardless of how much work you have put into outlining.

> Always outline in advance, a rough outline to think out your original, basic idea, refined into a more detailed outline after you have collected all your data.

ORGANIZATION, LEADS, AND BRIDGES

The part of writing that is often the most difficult challenge to meet, even for experienced professional writers, is organization—determining, that is, in what order to present the information. One reason for the difficulty is that there are many possible ways to organize information, and it is not always easy to decide which is the best one for your purposes. Some possible sequences of presentation (certainly not all), depending on the material, your reader, and your purposes in writing it, are these:

- ✔ Chronological or historical, from beginning to present.
- ✔ Reverse chronological tracing from present back to beginning.
- ✔ From smallest to largest.
- ✔ From largest to smallest.
- ✔ From effect to cause.
- ✔ From cause to effect.
- ✔ From least important to most important.
- ✔ From most important to least important.
- ✔ From the general to the specific.
- ✔ From the specific to the general.
- ✔ News style.

As you can see, many sequences or patterns of presentation have two opposite sides. You can use either side of the one you select as most suitable. If you are writing a newsletter and reporting news of some sort, you may find it easiest to use the journalistic inverted pyramid, in which you sum up the item briefly in a lead sentence that identifies what, who, when, where, and how, and then goes on to provide details. The advantage of using this style is that it helps you fit the copy to whatever space you have available because you can cut off the story at any point and still have a complete account. But you can write a news story as a feature, using another approach than the pyramidal one. In that case, you have to decide what is the best organization, considering your purpose overall, but also with regard to what is a compelling or interesting lead.

> Organizing your information is a most important part of writing, but to choose the best organization, you must have a clear idea of who your reader is and what you are trying to do for the reader.

For me (and for many other writers), my lead is to guide me, as well as my reader. It helps me remember where I started out to go. But it also serves a very useful purpose in helping me plan my organization. I try to find the key idea and incorporate that in the lead, and that search for the key idea and how to introduce it is a stimulant to me in my planning.

> All writing begins with a lead, an introduction that tells the reader where you are going and serves you as a planning tool and guide also. Use the lead in that way, too.

Using a lead is a method that is widely used in writing articles, and the organization is often dictated by the lead. You can't choose an attention-getting and interest-commanding lead and then abruptly abandon it. Your lead, the item you use first, not only rivets the reader's attention, it is a commitment and defines where you are going. For example, I began an introduction to government contracting with a statement that the government paid me $6,000 to answer their mail. That was only the first part of the lead.

I had to follow that sentence up with something that would complete the lead and tell the reader where we were going.

I had choices. I could use that statement as the beginning of a lead that would take us in any of several directions, such as these:

- ✔ Government contracts are open to anyone, even self-employed individuals.
- ✔ The government awards many novel contracts.
- ✔ The government needs all kinds of help.
- ✔ The government contracts for services, as well as for goods.

What I cannot do after that first sentence is go abruptly to an entirely unrelated subject, such as multimillion-dollar defense contracts. Yet, I can do so if I provide the linkage by saying something along the lines of, "Of course that does not compare with a $240 million contract awarded at the time to Boeing, although both were time and material contracts." That would permit me to shape the lead as one that would go on to introduce or discuss the kinds of contracts the government issues, the wide variety in the sizes of government projects, the opportunities for very small businesses, or even some other variations. the point is that you must provide a logical linkage or transition to whatever is to follow. (Writers often refer to such a linkage or transition as a "bridge," which it is.) Otherwise, if you switch abruptly from one subject to another without a bridge that helps the reader follow your thinking, you will probably confuse the reader, as many television dramas do when they do not provide clear enough bridges from one scene to the next.

Attend to this in all your writing. Whenever you introduce a new subject, help the reader follow you by providing bridges, which are also leads to the new subjects. I once had an editorial assistant who could detect and identify abrupt switches in subject, but who lacked the inventiveness to write suitable bridges. I had her simply mark such switches in the manuscript and then assigned a writer (sometimes myself) to insert suitable bridges.

> A most important aspect in writing is continuity of thought. You provide that to both the reader and yourself by using bridges to make transitions from one subject to the next. Be sure to provide them.

The length of a lead is in some proportion to the size of what is being introduced. The lead to a paragraph is normally the first sentence of the paragraph. The lead to an article is probably a full paragraph. The lead to a book is fairly lengthy, maybe an entire chapter. In writing one of my earliest books, my lead for the book was 50 typewritten pages long. By the time I had finished writing it on my typewriter (long before the personal computer arrived in the marketplace), I saw that it had not taken me where I wanted to go, but I now knew what my lead should be. I therefore scrapped it, all 50 pages consigned to the wastebasket with great reluctance and great pain, and started over. (It proved worth it. The book was a success.)

MORE MYTHOLOGY

Among the myths about writing is the notion that simple, easy to follow and understand writing is made up of short sentences and short words. The truth is that an article or book that consisted exclusively of short sentences would make a great soporific, a threat to the sleeping-pill market. Skillfully written sentences are easy to read and understand, regardless of length, and interesting writing includes sentences of varying lengths, some quite short, others quite long. A long sentence that presents related ideas in a logical sequence and with words in common use is not at all hard to read and understand. But when is a long sentence a long sentence? A sentence is terminated with a period, whereupon the next sentence is undertaken, but there are several ways to create stops in a long sentence so that its effect is the same as that of a string of short sentences while the train of thought is not interrupted. The stops are signs to the reader to pause momentarily to digest what has gone before, but also to note that the thought is not yet completed. Those shorter stops that can be used within a sentence include thoughts or comments within parentheses and dashes or separated by colons or semicolons. Take note of the many, many ways in which these are used by other writers.

The injunction to use short words, especially words of only one or two syllables, is equally misleading. "The earth is an oblate spheroid" is a short sentence, using short words. No word in it has more than two syllables or more than eight letters, and most of the words have only one syllable. But is it an easy sentence for the average person to understand? Or is a longer sentence with longer words—"The earth is shaped like an orange, round but slightly flattened at the top and bottom"—easier to follow? The difference is, of course, that the longer sentence uses images with which we all are familiar. (Semanticists would speak of "referents," but there is no need to get technical about such a simple idea as favoring words of everyday familiarity.)

> "Short," as used to recommend the nature of words and sentences to be employed in writing, is a word of indefinite meaning. It is most helpful when translated into practical terms.

PURPLE PROSE AND OTHER BAD WRITING

Probably the hallmark of bad writing is what has come to be called purple prose. Many individuals believe such writing to constitute literary elegance and great mastery of language in written expression. It is not easy to define purple prose, because it requires trying to understand the mind-set of the writer. However, I would define purple prose as language that parades a pompous or pretentious attitude, a kind of swagger that the writer apparently believes is evidence of a superior intellect. It is characterized by labored efforts to make dramatic statements and the free use of uncommon words, preferable those of great length, signifying a policy of never using a simple, common word where a complex, little-known word can be used instead.

Often, purple prose shares the characteristics of what is known as gobbledygook, a style of writing that emerges all too often from government offices and other bureaucratic institutions. That kind of writing is relatively easy to define and describe. In a word, it is writing that says nothing and requires many words to do so. That is easily revealed when you analyze the writing and try to restate it in shorter, more direct terms. The more you try to extract the central meaning, the more you find the task impossible, until you realize that the writer was simply tap dancing around the subject evasively, probably deceiving even him- or herself into believing that he or she has made an elegant statement because of the large number of words used. The test of such writing is editing it into a simple statement. It is normally not possible to do so.

Beware of becoming guilty of creating purple prose, gobbledygook, and other forms of bad writing and nonwriting. You can easily test your own writing and detect self-deception when you edit it and try to boil it down to a simple, factual statement.

Glossary

Introductory Note: A Special Caution

This glossary is written especially for the independent sales consultant. That is, all definitions are in terms of reference to independent consulting, and may have other meanings when applied to the business world at large.

acceptance obligatory condition of contracts in which one party accepts the other's offer.

accounting keeping track of all the money, in and out of the venture, and using that information as a basis for monitoring the health of the business and making management decisions, as well as paying taxes.

agreement verbal or written statement between two or more parties that can become a legally binding contract if it meets the five standard requirements.

ancillary services additional consulting services such as publishing newsletters and special reports, and presenting seminars.

arbitration method of resolving disputes through the services of a third party, outside the courts and law, accepted by the disputants to help find a basis for settling.

assignment transferring title of an asset, such as a receivable, to another party for a consideration.

billing rates standard rates charged clients per hour or per day for consulting services; other rates may exist for ancillary services.

boilerplate standard copy, as language for a clause used commonly.

broker one who arranges transactions for a commission or other compensation; also one supplying temporaries, in which case may also be referred to sardonically as a "job shop," "body shop," or supplier of "warm bodies."

capital-intensive business operations dependent primarily on capital investment and availability.

capital item an item, usually one with relatively long life, costing more than a figure set arbitrarily by the business owner as the defining point for all capital items.

cash flow the continuous availability of cash, as distinct from receivables.

cash flow management the methods and procedures used to establish and maintain the availability of ready cash for normal operating expenses.

change a change in requirement or other element that requires an amendment to the contract.

clauses sections of a contract that are supplementary agreements on peripheral, but important, interests of one party or the other.

competent adult and of normal intelligence; mandatory condition of both parties to make an agreement a legally binding contract.

concentration first step in inducing ideas by intense conscious effort to consider all ideas remotely possible.

confidential characteristic of information that one holds to be private property.

conflict of interest having an interest that is in opposition to your obligation to your client and may therefore color your judgment and make it difficult for you to be objective and ethical.

consideration that which changes hands as payment for exchange, usually paid by the party expressing acceptance of an offer; obligatory element in contracts.

consulting a special way to practice a profession by using one's special skills and knowledge to help clients solve problems.

contract agreement, verbal or written, meeting five conditions required to be legally binding contract.

contract amendment changes in contract, usually written, agreed to by both parties.

contract professional individual who normally works as a temporary.

conventional wisdom that which is believed to be generally true and valuable as a guideline.

copywriting writing advertising and promotional copy, or sell copy.

corporation artificial entity, recognized by the state, with certain benefits, such as limited liability, and certain obligations, such as paying taxes and keeping records.

creativity ability to solve problems and develop new ideas through concentration, incubation, and inspiration.

cyberspace the hypothetical space in which electronic communication and related activities of business take place, principally on the Internet.

d/b/a (doing business as) organization or individual doing business under an assumed name.

direct labor labor applied directly to client's work, costs of which are billable to client.

discounting paper selling receivables as assets at a discounted rate to banks or other lenders.

engineering change notice (ECN) a form used by most engineering offices to document a change.

factor one who buys receivables at a higher discounted rate than banks or other lenders.

flowchart chart showing sequential steps and interrelationships of various procedures or phases in the conduct of a project; useful for estimating, planning, and explaining projects to clients.

home office office in your home, using dedicated space.

incubation second step in inducing ideas and turning quest over to subconscious by dismissing subject entirely and turning to other activities, including relaxing ones.

independent consultant one who practices his or her career activity in a special mode, helping clients solve problems for which the consultant is especially fitted as an expert specialist.

independent contractor (IC) consultant who enters into contracts directly with clients, rather than via brokers, and works as a 1099 rather than as a W-2.

indirect labor labor not billable directly to clients, the costs of which are recovered in the overhead charge.

inspiration third step in inducing ideas by receiving sudden input from subconscious.

instrument written legal document, such as a will, contract, or deed.

Internet like cyberspace, that world of electronic communications and business transactions.

investment capital money used or required to start the business.

labor-intensive business activity selling direct labor as a major commodity and cost item.

local area network (LAN) interconnected computers within a building or suite of offices.

marketing all activities leading to and including making sales.

market niches special market segments selected as targets because of some distinctive characteristic.

mythology common beliefs that either are old wives' tales or are based on a tiny seed of fact, such as a single historical instance.

network the string of friends, acquaintances, and others you develop who know you and of you, and pass the word along to others.

networking creating a network; raising your visibility and enhancing your professional image through activities aimed to do these things, such as word-of-mouth advertising and publicity.

network maintenance continuous activity to keep your visibility high and your image what you want it to be by reminders and replacement of losses in network.

newsgroups many thousands of electronic communications and discussion groups, using e-mail and resembling electronic bulletin boards of pre-Internet days.

niche program program or special service that attracts so many participants that it becomes a market niche of its own, a private niche.

offer obligatory condition of contracts in which one party makes an offer.

operating capital money needed for day-to-day expenses and operating costs.

overhead indirect costs such as rent, heat, light, and indirect labor.

party one individual or organization entering into a contract.

payable bill received or money due someone, listed on books but not yet paid.

positioning shaping your image to how you wish clients to perceive you and what you offer—what you *do* for clients.

premises a physical location.

professional ethics a code of proper behavior and standards for independent consultants.

professional image how you are generally perceived as a professional expert who consults.

progress payments partial payments of the entire fee, paid at stated points in the progress of the work.

proposal an offer, usually (but not always) written, to enter into contract, presenting a plan and price.

proposal consultant one who offers a special service of sales consulting, helping clients create proposals and/or train their own staffs in proposal writing.

proprietary of ownership or owned by, as in proprietary information.

publicity informal name for public relations (PR); free advertising.

public relations (PR) activities to maintain an individual's or organization's visibility and image at most desirable levels; also referred to as publicity.

purchase order an agreement that is normally an informal contract.

receivable money due and listed on books but not yet received.

request for proposal (RFP) an invitation to compete for a contract to satisfy a stated requirement of the requester.

retainer nonreturnable fee or advance deposit to start consultant doing work called for.

sales converting prospects to clients and winning contracts.

sales consulting using expert sales skills and knowledge to help clients solve sales problems.

sell copy anything written to sell something; copywriting.

seminar a special training session involving one or more speakers for a period of not more than a few days.

service niche a segment of all the services possible selected as one's specialty.

sole proprietorship the sole ownership and control of a business venture, with all assets and liabilities those of the proprietor.

specifications precise and complete details of what is to be done and results required in both qualitative and quantitative terms.

1099 form issued to independent contractor by client listing total sum paid to independent contractor during the year; also term used to identify consultant informally as independent contractor, filing tax forms as independent business.

time and material contract a contract in which one is paid for his or her time at an agreed-upon rate and reimbursed for all materials used.

20 questions twenty points the IRS uses to judge whether a consultant is or is not legally a temporary employee.

USP a distinctive feature of one's product, service, or offer.

virtual corporation group of independent consultants who agree to work cooperatively on projects requiring teams of consultants with various specialties.

visibility the degree to which you are known as a consultant specialist.

win-lose negotiating negotiating to try to win everything possible.

win-win negotiating negotiating to try to reach compromises on all disputes that will satisfy both parties that they reached a fair exchange.

World Wide Web commonly accepted as part of the Internet and devoted primarily to business; casually referred to as the Web.

W-2 form required to be issued to employees; term used to designate working status of consultant as temporary employee, rather than independent contractor.

zoning laws statutes forbidding conduct of business in areas zoned by local government as for residential use only, as in private homes in such areas.

Index